MORE
90-Minute Quilts

20+ Quick and Easy Projects with Triangles and Squares

Meryl Ann Butler

kp

CINCINNATI, OHIO

Other fine Krause Publications titles are available from your local bookstore, craft supply store, online retailer or visit our website at www.fwmedia.com.

15   14   13   12   11   5   4   3   2   1

DISTRIBUTED IN CANADA BY FRASER DIRECT
100 Armstrong Avenue
Georgetown, ON, Canada L7G 5S4
Tel: (905) 877-4411

DISTRIBUTED IN THE U.K. AND EUROPE BY F+W MEDIA INTERNATIONAL
Brunel House, Newton Abbot, Devon, TQ12 4PU, England
Tel: (+44) 1626 323200, Fax: (+44) 1626 323319
Email: postmaster@davidandcharles.co.uk

DISTRIBUTED IN AUSTRALIA BY CAPRICORN LINK
P.O. Box 704, S. Windsor NSW, 2756 Australia
Tel: (02) 4577-3555

Library of Congress Cataloging-in-Publication Data

Butler, Meryl Ann.
 More 90-minute quilts : 20+ quick and easy projects with triangles and squares / author, Meryl Ann Butler.
     p. cm.
 Includes index.
 ISBN-13: 978-1-4402-1407-3 (hardcover : alk. paper)
 ISBN-10: 1-4402-1407-7 (hardcover : alk. paper)
1. Patchwork quilts. 2. Quilting--Patterns. 3. Triangle in art.
4. Square in art. I. Title.
 TT835.B8953 2011
 746.46'041--dc22
                          2010037147

WHO DID WHAT

Edited by Kelly Biscopink

Designed by Steven Peters

Production by Greg Nock

Photography by Christine Polomsky

Illustrated by Ron Carboni

METRIC CONVERSION CHART

To convert	to	multiply by
Inches	Centimeters	2.54
Centimeters	Inches	0.4
Feet	Centimeters	30.5
Centimeters	Feet	0.03
Yards	Meters	0.9
Meters	Yards	1.1

Dedication

- To Dad in appreciation of far too many things to list here, but especially of the fun we have had together lately
- To my elementary school art teacher, Doris Rogers, and to my high school English teacher, Lee Smith—your commitments to excellence and creativity have inspired me for decades beyond my school years
- To my kids, grand young'uns and other friends and family who have been such enthusiastic recipients of my 90-Minute Quilts
- To my students who inspire me to be the best teacher I can be
- And to the ever-increasing expression of the creative spirit within us all which, when nurtured, showers us with an abundant cascade of joy and well-being!

Acknowledgments of Appreciation

- First, I extend my heartfelt thanks to Sarah's Thimble Quilt Shoppe where most of the quilts seen in these pages were created. It is only with the Shoppe's generosity in providing the space in which to create that the dream of this book became a reality.
- Thank you to all the companies listed in the Resources Section (page 154) that offered advice, assistance and products for the projects in this book.
- I continue to be appreciative to Bernina of America and Pfaff for their gracious assistance in my projects over the years.
- I also appreciate the extra fast, "beyond-the-call-of-duty" service of both TrainFabrics (for the IN TRAINING quilt fabrics on page 140) and AbbiMays (for the flannel backing used in the GIVE 'EM SOMETHING TO TALK ABOUT quilt on page 53).
- I am delighted to acknowledge, with appreciation, the work of guest contributors elinor peace bailey (a doll goddess who spells her name in all lower-case letters), Susan Deal, Carole Dull, teen contributors Abigail Fenn and Hayley Keon, and the Girl Scouts of Troop 2286. Their work added a great deal of charm and inspiration to these pages.
- To my friend, Trish Schmiedl, who is an amazing digitizer and who translated my sketches into beautiful machine embroidery designs for the Aztec Dreams Shawl (page 142).
- My heartfelt thanks goes to the divine quilter goddesses who stitched up some of the early experimental projects, as well as many of the projects that appear in this book: Carole Dull, Robin Fenn, Abby Geddes, Gloria Hurban, Peggy Jebavy, Mary Menzer, Sarah Norman, Cynthia Rudy, Deborah Renfrow, Adelaide Rush, Barbara Sheipe and Kathy Thompson. Their attention to detail and creative suggestions added a great deal to the flavor of this book, and I pay homage with gorgeous garlands of thanks at their feet.
- I joyfully extend appreciation to Jerry and Esther Hicks, Norma Eckroate, Wendy Elwell and the rest of my uncannily creative cohorts for an eclectic range of innovative inspiration on this "hands up in the air, living on the edge, hollerin' at the top of our lungs" white-water-rapids ride down the stream of life. It's a joy to romp with you!
- I thank all those at Krause Publications who have extended their helpful hands in the birth process of this book, including acquisitions editor Christine Doyle, designer Steven Peters, production coordinator Greg Nock, photographer Christine Polomsky and illustrator Ron Carboni.
- And I appreciatively acknowledge my fabulous editor, Kelly Biscopink. When I was first given her name, I thought, "She must be the perfect editor for my book because her name has two of my favorite colors in it!" And my first impression has proven, to my deep delight, to be absolutely true.

Contents

A note from the author . . .

My 90-Minute Quilt techniques offer fun, fast and easy ways for quilters with busy lives to get projects done in record time. At last there's a way to get that crib quilt finished before the new baby leaves for college! And when making community service quilts, I can happily stitch up several in a day, allowing me to contribute to charity but still have time to devote to my more complex projects.

The name for these techniques comes from the 90 minutes of stitching time it takes to sew the basic 30" x 41" baby quilt. This includes piecing, quilting and binding, with a built-in rod pocket for hanging. If you haven't made one before, expect to spend some time digesting the instructions. But before you know it, you'll be speeding along, finishing projects before you are tired of looking at them.

In this sequel to *90-Minute Quilts: 15+ Projects You Can Stitch in an Afternoon*, half-square triangle units have been included, in addition to the squares used in the basic baby quilts. This greatly expands the design possibilities! While these more complex projects require added stitching, and therefore a little more time, additional fast options are offered.

When quilts are created for emotional comfort, it's helpful to be able to complete one quickly. I developed these methods when my young daughter and I were healing from the loss of her father. These techniques enabled her to finish a quilt within her attention span, and she was rewarded with a sense of comfort, accomplishment and the opportunity to exhibit her quilt in my guild's show.

So whether you start with the signature baby quilt or with a more complex project, I hope you have fun dancing through the delights of stitching and the satisfaction of speedy, successful quilts!

Love,
Meryl Ann

Section One

GETTING STARTED

More *90-Minute Quilts* offers new fast and easy techniques you can use to finish projects quickly. The simplest version of the original 90-Minute Quilt process requires about an hour and a half of sewing time for piecing, quilting and binding, and it inspired the name of this group of techniques.

This book includes the original process and also introduces more complex quilts based on the same methods. While these new quilts may take proportionately more time to complete, they are still some of the fastest quilts you will ever whip up!

Contemporary stitchers who have less time to quilt than grandma had can maximize their sewing time with clever techniques and innovative devices.

90-MINUTE TIME-SAVING TOOLS

The tools and notions showcased in this chapter enhance the efficiency of quilting processes such as measuring, cutting and pressing. If you are an experienced quilter, you probably have most of these items already. If you are new to quilting, this section lists the basic tools needed and offers information on items you'll want to add to your collection of time-saving devices.

CUTTING AND MEASURING TOOLS

Cutting Mats

For most projects in this book, a cutting mat at least 18" × 24" is required; a larger one, such as 24" × 36", is even better. For larger projects, a 23" × 70" mat is a great help when trimming because it gives accurate measurements up to 70".

A revolving mat is useful for fussy-cutting and trimming. If you don't have one yet, try placing a small mat on top of a larger mat and rotate as needed to create your own temporary revolving mat.

Rotary Cutters

Rotary cutters are available in a variety of shapes and sizes. Cutters with 60mm or 45mm blades and ergonomic handles offer comfort when cutting fabric for lots of quilts. Save "nonfavorite" rotary cutters for blades that become too dull for cutting fabric. Use them for cutting paper (especially when wrapping lots of gifts) and template material.

Scissors and Thread Snips

Scissors are essential for trimming fabrics and threads. Keep a pair of small scissors or thread snips by the machine or in a chatelaine for snipping threads quickly as you sew. Spring-action scissors may be easier for arthritic hands to use.

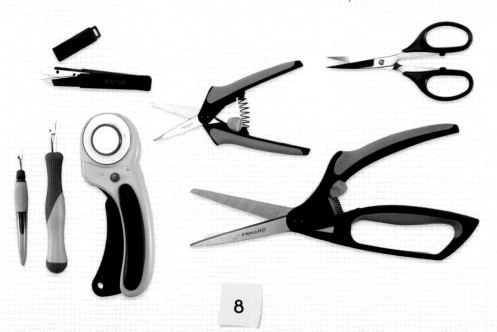

Rulers

Clear plastic, nonslip rulers are essential for accurate cutting. A basic 6" × 24" ruler is useful for all projects, and an 8½" × 24" is great for projects with squares that are larger than 6 inches. Having a wide variety of other rulers can offer valuable time savings when cutting—especially square rulers that are the exact size of the squares you are cutting. I collect them all! Refer to the Ruler Information chart on page 157 for a list of useful sizes.

InvisiGrip can be added to the underside of rulers that don't have a non-slip feature to help stabilize them when cutting. A hem gauge that locks in place is a handy, time-saving tool for accurately measuring the width of bindings and narrow borders. I like Nancy Zieman's 5-in-1 Sliding Gauge (shown at right).

Storing frequently used rulers upright in a slotted wooden rack and within easy reach saves time, too. An old mailbox, like the one shown, makes a perfect holder for longer rulers.

Marking Rulers for Repetitive Cutting

Transparent, fluorescent tape that temporarily adheres to the ruler highlights selected cutting lines, making it faster to relocate the lines during repetitive cutting. Small postable notes can also be used for this. Removable tape, found in office supply stores, is another useful way to temporarily mark a ruler when fussy-cutting repetitive motifs.

Pins and Pincushions

Magnetic and wrist pincushions save time in the pinning process. Glass heads won't melt if hit by the iron. Flat flower-head pins won't unbalance a ruler placed on top of them during cutting. Quilters' curved safety pins take a little longer to use but are safer, especially when working with young quilters.

For even more efficiency, use separate magnetic pincushions for each different type of pin so you don't have to spend time digging out the best pin for the job!

Chalk and Markers

Powdered chalk markers come in a variety of colors and are an effective way to mark your project. Permanent marking pens, such as Micron and Sharpie, are useful for coloring over thread mistakes and for marking fabric within seam allowances.

Viewing Window

Cut a square window in a piece of cardboard to preview fussy-cut motifs. (Cut the hole ½" smaller than the size of the cut squares to allow for the ¼" seam allowances.)

Fusible Webbing

Pressure-sensitive, double-stick, fusible webbing allows fine-tuning because it is repositionable prior to ironing. Sheets of fusible webbing may be used in the machine appliqué process (such as for the eye on SWEET SCOTTIE on page 80).

Use ½" or ¼" wide double-stick fusible web tape as an efficient way to baste self-binding without pinning.

Pressing Helpers

A mini iron is an easy way to press seams quickly. Lightweight fabric press cloths and fiberglass or Teflon pressing sheets are essential to protect specialty fabrics from heat and to keep fusible web debris from sticking to the iron or other surfaces.

Put that empty space under your ironing board to good use by hanging a circular ruler holder under your ironing board to hold press cloths for convenient retrieval when pressing. I use the one from June Tailor.

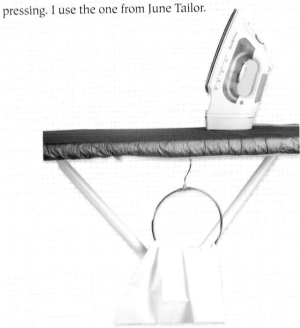

Flat Surface for Layout

A 40" × 72" folding cardboard cutting board, a flannel board or a portable design wall provide large, flat surfaces for laying out quilt squares. If you are making your own flannel board, adhere a neutral color of flannel such as gray, taupe or tan to a foamcore board in the size you prefer. White or black backgrounds can create optical illusions: A white background makes fabrics appear darker by contrast, and a black background makes fabrics appear lighter. A middle-value gray background offers the least visual interference and allows you to see color and value relationships unencumbered.

STORAGE AND CARE

Store extra fabric squares and strips in plastic or archival-grade cardboard storage boxes large enough so that the pieces lie flat. These pieces can be organized by size, motif, theme and color. Consider cutting your favorite sizes from select fabrics as you purchase them in order to build a stash of pre-cut squares that are ready when inspiration strikes!

Selecting Fabric Colors

Color has three properties: hue, value and saturation. (Saturation may also be called chroma or intensity.)

Hue

Hue is the name of the color family: red, red-orange, orange, yellow-orange, yellow, yellow-green, green, blue-green, blue, blue-violet, violet and red-violet. Each color family includes colors of different values, from lighter to darker. For instance, peach and rust are in the orange family, and olive and kiwi are in the yellow-green family. Warm hues of red, orange, yellow and yellow-green tend to advance from the design surface, and cool hues of green, blue-green, blue, blue-violet and violet tend to recede. A color wheel is a useful tool for corralling all those zillions of colors into hue categories.

Color temperature can enhance the atmosphere and mood of your quilt design. Warm hues generally feel more engaging, emotive and energetic, and cool hues feel more meditative, restful and introspective. For instance, the warm reds and yellows in the Feng Shui Good Luck wall hanging (page 70) feel more active than the cool blues and greens in the Make It Green for Baby! quilt (page 76).

Value

Value refers to the lightness or darkness of a color. Some of the projects in this book were designed as an opportunity to explore value relationships, including A Passion for Plum (page 106), Celebrate! (page 102) and Sail Away, Monet (page 118).

The Garden Trellis quilt (page 138) features dark squares against white triangles, and the In Training quilt variation (page 140) features lighter squares against black triangles. This switch in values creates a very different look, even though the quilt design is exactly the same. Referring to a value scale can help you assign values to your fabrics.

Saturation

Saturation, also called intensity or chroma, refers to the purity of the hue. High-intensity colors are pure, saturated rainbow colors. Serengeti Rainbows (page 48) and Quilt of Many Colors (page 62) both feature highly saturated colors.

Lower-intensity colors are more complex because they have white, black or gray mixed into the intense hue. These are often referred to as "tonal" or "soft" colors.

A Passion for Plum (page 106) is lower intensity, or low chroma, because the colors are all "shades," which are produced by adding black to pure hues. Magical Meadows (page 52) has lower saturation because most of the colors are "tints," which are produced by adding whites to pure hues. In Celebrate! (page 102), the colors are lower saturation because most are "tones," which are produced by adding gray to pure hues. In these three examples, the pure, saturated hues are all diffused by the addition of a dark, medium or light value.

The study of color can be very complex—some people study it for a lifetime! But simply noticing hue, value and chroma will train your eye and give you new confidence in using color in your quilts.

FABRICS, BATTING AND THREADS

Fabrics

One hundred percent cotton fabrics are used in all the projects in this book except those that specify specialty fabrics, such as silk. I recommend high-quality quilters' fabrics for best results.

Most 90-Minute Quilts are made with a cotton flannel backing and self-binding. Using flannel for the backing and self-binding makes the stitching process faster because the fabrics tend to stay in place with less pinning needed. Flannel also gives a bit more body to a quilt, which is especially good for a wall hanging. And flannel feels so cozy on the back and the edges of a quilt!

When selecting a flannel backing/binding, choose a color that will coordinate with the other fabrics in the quilt. Random or all-over "tossed" prints with medium to small motifs or tonal prints are best. Stripes, plaids, obvious geometric prints and one-way designs are not suitable for self-binding since they draw attention to any mis-measurement. Other recommended backings include organic cotton fleece, microfiber plush (such as Minkee) and silk noil.

Prewashing Fabric

Prewashing fabric is recommended. Always prewash flannel and silk noil at least once before cutting and stitching, as both typically shrink. Noil may need to be prewashed twice, as it may continue to shrink significantly the second time it is washed and dried. My new fabrics go directly to the laundry room after purchasing because I prefer to remove the sizing chemicals before adding the fabrics to my studio. I make rare exceptions when teaching children how to sew, if the particular fabric is more easily manageable before washing, or for a project not likely to be used next to the skin. I recommend using a biodegradable cleanser containing no phosphates or bleach for washing fabric and quilts.

I don't prewash organic fabrics, but I recommend washing your completed organic quilt with a natural biodegradable and hypoallergenic concentrate with no phosphates or chlorine, such as Shaklee Get Clean Fresh Laundry Concentrate. For most hand-dyed fabrics, I recommend pre-washing in Synthrapol or a similar product.

When machine washing quarter yards or other small pieces of fabric, place them in a zippered lingerie bag and wash on the gentle cycle to prevent excessive tangling and unraveling.

Batting

Battings come in a wide variety of weights and styles. When selecting batting, consider the size of the squares in your project and how close you will make your quilting stitches. Check the batting packaging or contact the manufacturer to find out how far apart the batting can be quilted. When using a batting that requires stitches closer together than the size of the squares in the project, additional quilting may be required. Refer to the Batting Information chart on page 157 for additional details.

Choose battings with a flexible drape for doll quilts. Choose stiffer, denser battings for wall hangings or larger quilts. 90-Minute Quilts are perfect for trying out new battings before you commit to using them in a more complex project.

If the backing of a quilt is silk noil and you'd like to use batting, I recommend using lightweight cotton flannel fabric in place of batting to avoid bearding.

Polar fleece, cotton fleece and flannel can serve as batting and backing, giving the "quilt sandwich" only two layers instead of three. Using flannel or noil without batting creates a cuddly, summer-weight quilt.

Alpaca fleece is deliciously soft fleece. It has no lanolin (as wool does) and therefore does not require chemicals for removing the lanolin. It is nonallergenic and fireproof! (I admit I haven't spent much time worrying about what happens to an alpaca on fire. But, still, it's a relief to know!)

Meryl Ann has fun feeding the gregarious and hypoallergenic Aragon Alpacas in Eugene, Oregon.
(Photo courtesy of Ann Dockendorf)

Thread

Use good-quality, brand-name thread. Cheaper threads may fill your sewing machine with debris, making servicing necessary more often. Using a bobbin winder will lessen the number of times you must stop and reload your bobbin.

When using monofilament thread for quilting, experiment with your machine's top tension on a piece of scrap material. Then write the tension setting on the end of the spool so you'll always know what setting to use.

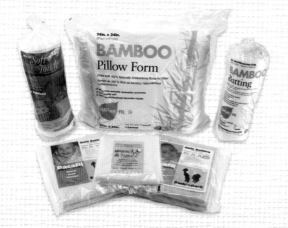

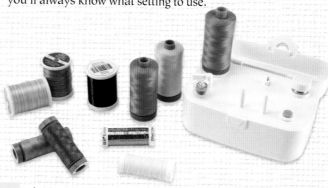

90-MINUTE TIME-SAVING TECHNIQUES

You will be referring to these sections for all the projects in this book. The colorful page edging will help you flip back to this section for easy reference.

PRESSING VS. IRONING

Pressing is an up-and-down motion: pick up the iron, set it down on the fabric and lift it again. The side-to-side movements in ironing may stretch fabrics. The project instructions in this book recommend pressing rather than ironing in order to preserve the accurate grain line, cut and shape of the fabric.

For the greatest accuracy in pressing, such as for half-square triangle units, first press the seam in the closed position just as it was sewn. This impresses the stitching threads into the weave of the fabric. Let the fabric cool a bit before opening it and pressing the seam allowance toward the darker fabric.

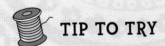

TIP TO TRY

When cutting a piece of batting from a larger piece, make a notation on a 3" × 5" index card of the size of the remaining piece of batting, and insert the card into the batting bag. This way, you can identify the size of the leftover batting without opening up the bag to measure!

ROTARY CUTTING

For the projects in this book, you will need long and square rulers, a rotary cutter and a cutting mat. Use removable tape or small postable notes to highlight the cutting line on the ruler for faster, more accurate cutting.

Fussy-cut your fabric when a specific motif needs to be framed in the square. Line up the center "x" markings on a square ruler of the appropriate size with the center of the motif. Then rotary cut around the ruler for a perfect fussy-cut square.

Fussy-cutting motifs can require more yardage than listed, depending on the motif size and the length of the repeat. Not sure if you have enough fabric to get all the motifs you need? Mark them all with chalk before cutting to make sure.

If your square ruler does not have "x" markings or if you are using a larger ruler than the required size, use removable tape to create your own temporary markings on the ruler.

The "fussy trimming" technique is used to create perfectly-sized, half-square triangle units. Line up the center diagonal line of the ruler along the seam, and trim for a perfect square.

CREATING FOUR-PATCH KALEIDOSCOPE UNITS

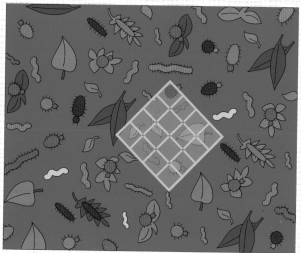

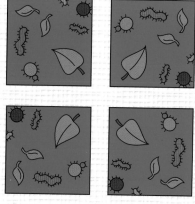

1 Position the ruler of the appropriate size over the selected motif. Adhere two to four pieces of frosted removable tape to the ruler over strategic areas of the motif. Trace these motif areas onto the tape with a fine-point permanent marker. Use these as guides to line up the ruler quickly and accurately when cutting additional squares of the same design.

2 Fussy-cut four identical squares slightly larger than needed from the motif selected. Arrange the set of four identical squares with the same area of the design positioned in the center of the Four-Patch, as shown. You may rotate the squares to achieve different looks. The overall look of the Four-Patch unit changes slightly after the seams are stitched.

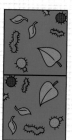
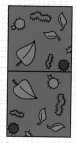
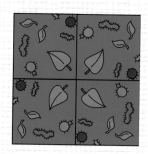

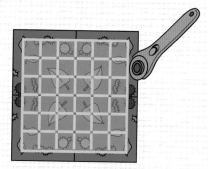

3 Stitch the two left-hand squares together and press the seam allowance up. Stitch the two right-hand squares together and press the seam allowance down. Nesting the seam allowances, stitch the two units together to create a Four-Patch. Press.

4 Place the Four-Patch on a rotating mat. Center an appropriately-sized square ruler on the Four-Patch, matching center and seam lines with the markings on the ruler. Trim the excess fabric to create a perfectly pieced kaleidoscope Four-Patch.

MAKING FOUR-PATCH SQUARES

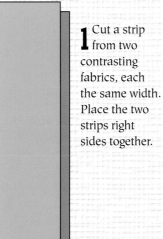

1 Cut a strip from two contrasting fabrics, each the same width. Place the two strips right sides together.

2 Sew a ¼" seam down one long side of the strips.

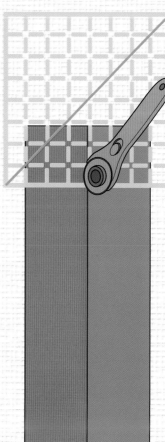

3 Open the strip set and press. Subcut the strip set into sections the width of the original strip.

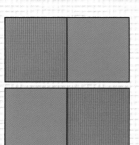

4 Place two of these strip sections together, with matching fabrics in opposing corners, to create a checkerboard.

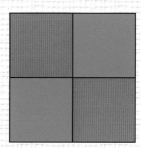

5 Place the strip sections right sides together, nesting the seams together. Join with a ¼" seam. Open and press.

Making Half-Square Triangle Units
Method #1

Use this method to make a small number of half-square triangle units when accuracy is more important than speed. For this method, squares are cut about 1" larger than the size of the finished block and do not have to be perfectly accurate, as they will be trimmed later. This is a great method for using all those miscut squares you receive in quilt-bee exchanges.

drawn line

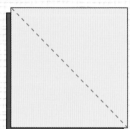

stitching lines

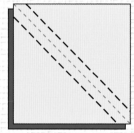

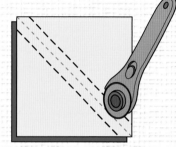

1 Cut a square from two contrasting fabrics, both 1" larger than the size of the finished half-square triangle unit. On the wrong side of one square, draw a diagonal line from one corner to the other. Place the two squares right sides together, lining up raw edges.

2 Stitch on each side of the drawn diagonal line, using a ¼" seam allowance.

3 Cut along the drawn line.

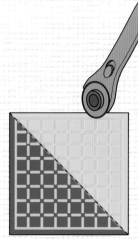

4 Press the square while it is still closed. Open the square, pressing the seam allowance toward the darker fabric. Press gently on the bias areas.

5 Line up the diagonal of the appropriately-sized square ruler on the seam line and fussy-cut around it to make a perfect square. A revolving mat is useful for trimming.

Making Half-Square Triangle Units
Method #2

Use this method to make a larger number of half-square triangle units from the same pair of fabrics.

1 Cut strips from two contrasting fabrics according to project instructions. Place the two strips right sides together.

2 Stitch along both long sides, creating a tube. Press to set the seams.

3 Line up the diagonal line on an appropriately sized ruler with the stitching line. Rotary cut along two sides. Place the ruler on the seam on the opposite side and repeat. Cut the required number of half-square triangle units.

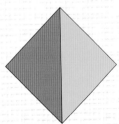

4 Open each half-square triangle unit, removing any small bit of stitching that may remain at the apex of the triangles. Press the seam allowance toward the darker fabric, pressing gently on the bias areas.

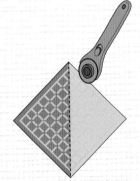

5 Line up the diagonal of the appropriately-sized square ruler on the seam line and fussy-trim to a perfect square.

Making Half-Square Triangle Units
Method #3

Use this method to make a small number of half-square triangle units when speed is more important than accuracy.

Cut a square from each of two contrasting fabrics, each ½" larger than the size of the finished half-square triangle unit measurement. Follow Steps 1–4 on page 17. The block will be the finished size without further trimming.

Making Half-Square Triangle Units
Method #4

Use this method to make 3-D half-square triangle units, as used in Sweet Scottie (page 80) and A Passion for Plum (page 106).

folding line

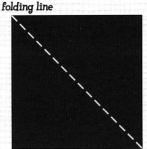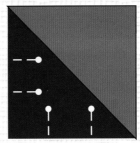

1 Each half-square triangle unit requires two squares of the same size. Fold one square in half diagonally with wrong sides together. Press carefully to avoid stretching; spray with water while pressing to create a crisp fold.

2 Place the folded square on top of the unfolded square and pin. When the pinned block is stitched to the adjacent squares, the half-square triangle will be secured. This produces a three-dimensional half-square triangle unit with a pocket effect.

Leapfrog Cutting Method

For speedy cutting of strips and squares for 90-Minute Quilts and other projects, use the "leapfrog method" of speed cutting. In this technique, you will place one ruler flush with another ruler; this is much faster and more accurate than trying to line up the ruler with lines on the mat or with the trimmed edge of the fabric. This is a particularly useful trick for sizes you cut frequently and for when you must cut a large number of squares, such as for a guild fabric exchange.

In the leapfrog cutting technique, the full width of the ruler determines the finished width of the strip or square. You will need a rotary cutter, a 24" × 36" mat and two rulers, each the desired strip/square width.

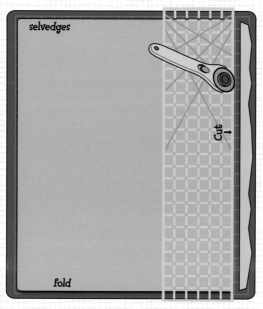

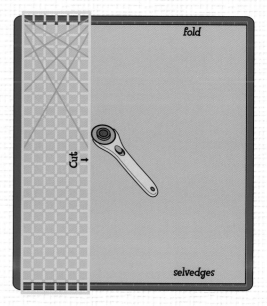

1 Position the cutting mat on a sturdy surface on which you can rotate the mat easily. Place the folded fabric in the center of the cutting mat, with the folded edge near you, and line it up with a horizontal line on the mat.

2 To trim the right edge of the fabric, line up the ruler with a vertical line on the mat. Holding the ruler steady, cut along the edge of the ruler, away from your body. Remove the waste while holding the ruler in place to keep your fabric lined up accurately on the mat.

3 Carefully rotate the mat with the fabric on it 180 degrees. Make sure the left-hand edge of the ruler is still lined up with the trimmed edge of the fabric. Holding the ruler firmly in place, cut along the right-hand edge of the ruler, cutting your first strip. *Do not remove the ruler or reposition the fabric.*

4 While continuing to hold the first ruler in place, use your other hand to position a second ruler to the right of it, lining it up flush with the first ruler. Make the second cut along the edge of this ruler.

5 Continue to hold the second ruler firmly. Pick up the first ruler and leapfrog it, placing it on the other side of the second ruler. Line it up flush. Make the third cut and carefully remove the rulers without shifting the fabric.

6 Rotate the mat with the fabric on it 90 degrees. Trim the selvedges evenly. If you are cutting strips, you are finished. If you are cutting squares, rotate the mat 180 degrees and repeat Steps 3–5 to sub-cut squares.

Note: Begin cutting your squares at the selvedge edge. Depending on the size of your squares, you may get a "bonus" square from the folded end of each strip.

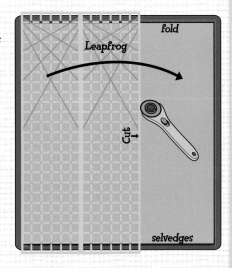

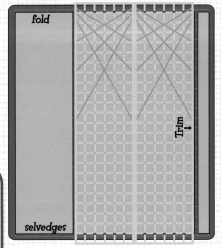

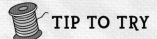

TIP TO TRY

Use three 6" × 24" rulers to create an 18" × 24" accordion-fold ruler that makes cutting fat quarters quick and accurate. This is helpful when preparing for a guild's fat-quarter fabric swap, for squaring up corners of larger quilts or just for making larger measurements accurately.

Place two 6" × 24" rulers next to each other and tape them together with clear package tape on the front of the rulers. Turn the taped duo upside down and place another ruler next to it, taping it on the back. Fold it accordion-style to store. Open it up for a 24" × 18" ruler for cutting fat quarters fast. The tape can be removed later, but I find it more convenient to permanently dedicate three of my older rulers for this.

LAYING OUT SQUARES

Arrange the squares on a flat design surface, such as a cutting board or flannel board, following the quilt layout shown for each project. Pin a postable note to the top square in each column, numbering them from left to right. For larger, more complex quilts, mark the top center of each square with chalk or permanent marker inside the seam allowance to make it easy to double-check the orientation as the squares are sewn together. Stack the squares in each column, being careful to keep them in proper orientation.

BUTTERFLY DELIGHT

35" x 44"
Sample stitched by Gloria Hurban.

In This Project: Fabrics by Kari Pearson for Quilting Treasures, Dan Morris' Phoebe flannel by Robert Kaufman; Fairfield's Nature-fil Bamboo Batting

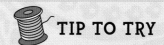 **TIP TO TRY**

If you like to do some of your pinning on the ironing board, slip a long ruler under the areas you are working on to prevent pinning your project to the ironing board cover.

22

Sewing the Squares

Note: I recommend using a walking foot or even-feed mechanism if available. All seam allowances are ¼" unless otherwise noted.

1 Positioning the stack of squares with the top of the stack toward the right makes it easier to keep the squares in the correct orientation as you pick them up to stitch pairs together. Chain-sew for speed, as well as to keep the stitched pairs in order.

2 Stitch the squares in Column 1 together, taking care to keep them in order and in the right orientation. Cotton squares tend to adhere to each other, and a walking foot or even feed will keep the fabric from slipping, so experienced sewers may not need to pin the squares together. If you do use pins, remove them as you stitch, or position them out of range of the needle. Leave the postable note with the column number pinned to the top square.

3 Repeat Step 2 for the remaining columns. Place each sewn column back onto the design surface in the appropriate position, checking to make sure each square is in the proper place.

4 Press the seam allowances down (away from the top square) on odd-numbered columns. Press the seam allowance up (toward the top square) on even-numbered columns. (Tip for remembering: The words *odd* and *down* both have a *d* in them.)

23

Prepare the Backing

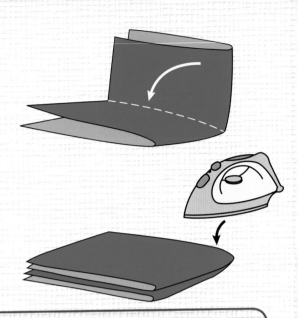

1 With the wrong sides together, fold the flannel backing in half, and in half again.

2 Press the corner folds lightly to mark the center.

3 Open, and place the backing right side down on a flat surface, smoothing out wrinkles with your hands.

4 If your quilt will contain batting, go to Adding the Batting (page 25). If not using batting, skip to Sewing the Columns (page 26).

VARIATION: PIECED BACKINGS FOR LARGER QUILTS

Note: If you don't want to piece the backing for larger quilts, use extra wide flannel yardage or a flannel sheet.

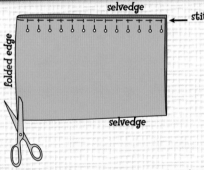

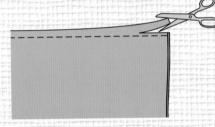

1 Fold the flannel yardage right sides together, lining up the selvedges.

2 Pin along one selvedge edge.

3 Stitch along the pinned selvedge with a ⅝" seam allowance. Cut through the fold.

4 Trim ⅜" off the stitched selvedge edge creating ¼" seam allowance.

5 Press the seam allowance open.

6 Trim the pieced flannel to the size needed. Offset the seam from the exact center of the quilt so the seam allowances from stitching the columns won't overlap this seam.

ADDING THE BATTING

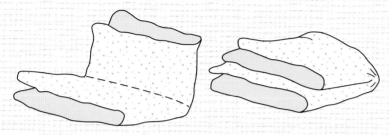

1 Fold the batting in half, and in half again.

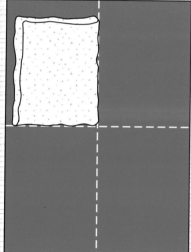 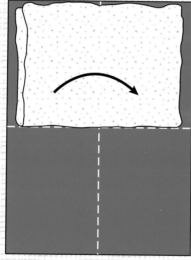 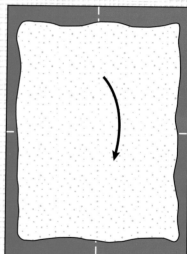

2 Line up the corner fold of the batting with the marked center of the flannel backing.

3 Unfold the batting and center it on the flannel backing. The batting and the flannel backing will not be exactly the same size—this is normal at this stage.

Sewing the Columns

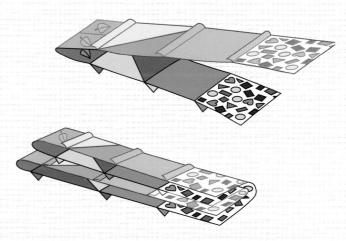

1 Lifting one corner of the backing/batting unit, insert a long pin through the pressed center marking of the flannel backing and up through the batting (if you are using it). The pin should be visible on the top of the batting.

2 Pick up the center column. (Projects with an even number of columns offer adjusted instructions for the placement of the first column.) Find the center of this column by folding it in half lengthwise with right sides together and then folding it in half again crosswise.

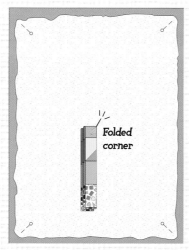

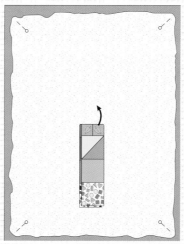

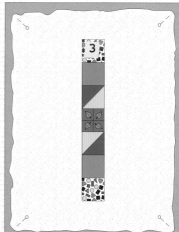

3 Line up the folded corner with the center pin.

4 Unfold the column once and remove the pin. Unfold again to center the column on the backing/batting unit.

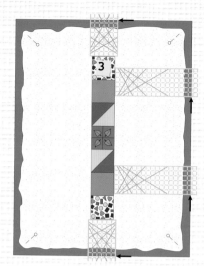

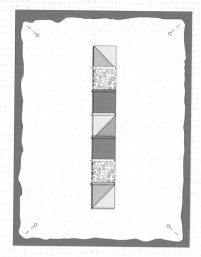

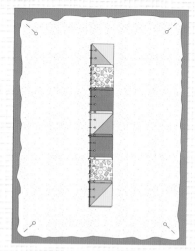

5 Measure from the edges of the column to the edges of the flannel backing to make sure the column is accurately centered on the backing/batting unit. Pin the column through the batting and backing.

6 Place the adjacent column with the next-lowest number on the center column, right sides together. In this example, Column 2 is placed over Column 3.

7 Pin along the left raw edges, nesting the seam allowances into each other like puzzle pieces. Pin through the visible seam allowances to secure them.

8 Insert bobbin thread to match the backing fabric. Use an even-feed foot or engage the even-feed function on your machine for the best results. Increase the stitch length slightly and stitch the columns together through the batting and backing using ¼" seam allowance unless otherwise instructed. Backstitch at the beginning and end of the seam. If prefered, tie knots instead of backstitching, reaching inside the quilt sandwich and pulling threads to the inside before tying them so knots will be hidden wherever possible.

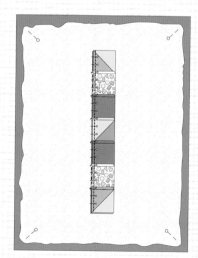

Note: Each time you begin sewing a column down, hold onto the thread tails for the first few stitches so that they don't bind up on the back of your quilt.

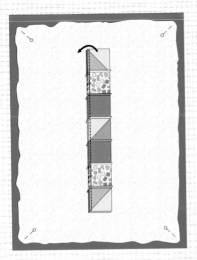

9 Check the stitching on the back of the quilt to make sure there are no unwanted tucks. Unpin and flip the stitched column open, smoothing it out. Press lightly if desired.

10 Check the stitching on the front of the quilt to make sure the seam was stitched accurately with no raw edges peeking through. Pin this column down flat through the backing and batting.

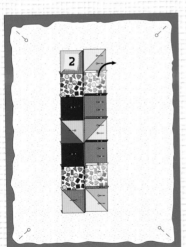

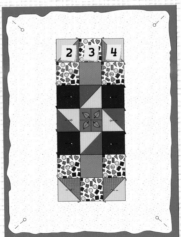

11 Repeat Steps 6–10 with the adjacent, larger-numbered column. In this example, it is Column 4.

12 Repeat Steps 6–10 with the remaining columns in order.

QUILTING THE PROJECT

The quilt top is already secured by the vertical seams, so extensive pinning is not necessary—pin only around the perimeter of the quilt. Stitching the columns together also begins the quilting process, so a 90-Minute Quilt is a perfect project for experimenting with various free-motion machine or long-arm quilting techniques. None of your recipients are likely to complain if a few experimental stitches seem out of whack—they'll only feel the love that went into it!

1 Remove the postable notes and discard them.

2 Smooth out and pin the corners and raw edges through all layers.

3 Thread the machine with thread that contrasts with the top, and load the bobbin with thread to match the backing. Start with a full bobbin. Lengthen the stitch slightly for quilting.

4 Quilt as desired or as suggested: Begin in any corner, backstitch (or plan to tie threads later) and machine quilt a straight diagonal line across each square.

First quilting path

5 Stitch to within ¼" of the raw edges on the outside squares. Leave the needle in the down position, raise the presser foot and pivot the quilt to reposition it. Lower the presser foot and continue quilting along the next diagonal.

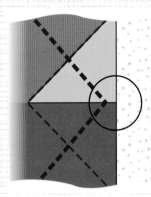

6 Backstitch (or tie threads) when you have completed the first pass at the opposite corner from where you started.

7 Begin the second pass at either remaining corner and continue as in Steps 4–6. Remove the pins.

Second quilting path

Adding Borders Courthouse-Steps Style

Note: If your project does not have borders, skip this section and go to Self-Binding on page 32.

1 Cut the border fabric strips as directed in the project instructions. For larger sizes, you may need to piece the borders.

2 Pin the border strips to the long sides of the quilt, matching the raw edges. At each end, extend the border strips at least ¼"–½" beyond the raw edges to allow for shifting of fabric when stitching. Trim excess fabric after stitching.

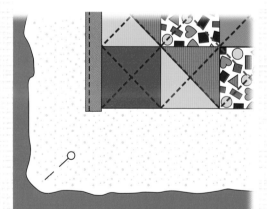

3 Stitch the border strips to the sides of the pieced quilt unit using a ¼" seam allowance. Backstitch at the beginning and end of each seam if desired. (In some instances, the directions may instruct you to add top and bottom borders first.)

4 Flip the border strips open and press. Press carefully avoiding contact with batting. The border may extend about ¼" past the edge of the quilted squares. Trim slightly if desired, but not too much! It's better to have a little excess fabric than not enough.

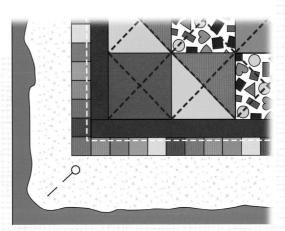

5 In the same manner, add the border strips to the top and bottom. If the quilt has an outer border, add it in the same manner.

6 *Optional*: Add a line or two of outline stitching on the inside of the border using the presser foot as a width guide. Start partway down one side, not in a corner. Backstitch at the beginning and end of the stitching or tie threads. Use the needle-down function to pivot at corners and, if available, use the markings on the presser foot to assist in gauging where to end the stitching lines at the corners. A chalk line at the quilt corners at a 45 degree angle will help you stitch accurate corners.

VARIATION: ADDING BORDERS LOG-CABIN STYLE

Moving in a clockwise pattern around the quilt, add one side border, followed by the top border, then the next side border, and finally the bottom border.

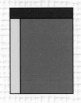
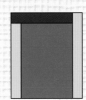
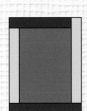

SELF-BINDING

1 Starting at the top of the quilt, rotary-cut the backing to the specified amount, usually 3½" from the raw edges of the borders. You will be cutting through some or all of the batting as well. Place transparent fluorescent tape (or two or three small postable notes) along the 3½" measuring line of your 6" × 24" ruler to help ensure accuracy. If desired, draw arrows on the tape to indicate the measuring line selected.

2 Repeat Step 1 to trim the bottom of the quilt and the two sides.

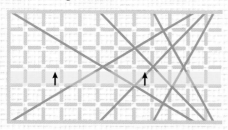

3 Fold the top "backing flap" backward, right sides together, ensuring that the flannel backing is folded securely away from the batting. Luckily, flannel will tend to stick to itself, which will help you in this step.

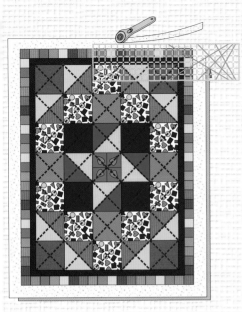

4 Trim the batting to the specified amount, usually 1¼" from the raw edge of the border, being sure the backing is folded securely away from the batting.

5 Flip the flannel backing back up.

6 Repeat Steps 3–5 on the bottom and sides of the quilt.

7 Press under the raw edge of the backing, wrong sides together, on both long sides. The amount to press under may vary from a generous ¼" to ⅜" depending on the thickness of the batting used.

Note: Before pressing, fold the raw edge in to determine which measurement works best for your quilt. For best results, use a locking sewing gauge for measuring. Once you have determined the best measurement for your quilt, use that same measurement consistently. The next fold (Step 8) will need to cover ¼"–⅜" of the raw edges.

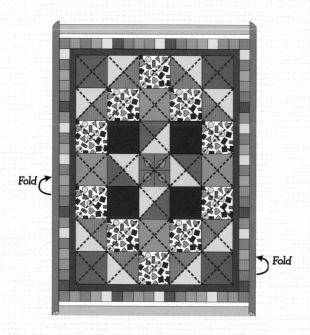

Fold ↻

Fold ↺

8 Fold the flannel over the batting to cover at least ¼" of the raw edges of the border. With a seam gauge, measure to make sure the width of the self-binding strip is the same all around the quilt. Press.

9 Baste with pins or pressure-sensitive fusible-web tape.

Fusible-web method: *Apply ½" or ¼" wide fusible-web tape to the underside of the self-binding. Position it about ⅛" in from edge of the fold so it straddles the raw edge, sealing it. Remove the paper backing and finger press in place. Check that all the raw edges are sufficiently covered. Measure, if desired. Press with an iron to bond permanently, using a press cloth or pressing sheet to protect the iron and ironing board from getting gunked up with wayward webbing.*

Pin-basting method: *Pin the self-binding in place very generously. Check that all raw edges are sufficiently covered.*

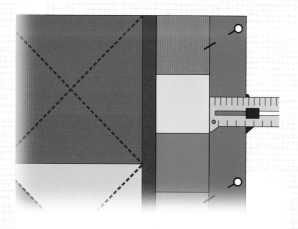

10 Use a locking seam gauge to make sure the self-binding is even all around the quilt.

Stitch ↓

Stitch ↑

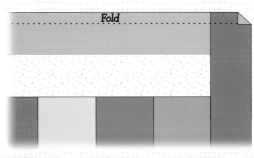

Fold

12 Repeat Steps 7–10 on the top and bottom, but after pressing the raw edges under, open them and fold the corners in, pressing again to make neat corners. Then stitch down the top and bottom binding as in Step 11.

11 Edgestitch the inside edge of the binding with thread that matches or contrasts with the backing/binding. (Edgestitching is topstitching within ¹⁄₁₆" of the edge of the fabric.) Check closely to make sure the raw edges underneath the binding were caught in the stitches. If some raw edges escaped being stitched, there's no need to rip out the whole seam—just "unsew" 2"–3" on each side of the offending area and repin. Be sure to overlap the edges sufficiently, and resew.

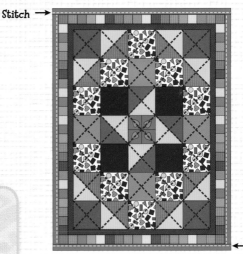

Stitch →

Stitch ←

TIP TO TRY

Stitching the top and bottom self-bindings after stitching the sides forms a self-casing for hanging the quilt. If you don't plan to hang your quilt, and you prefer a more finished edge, leave the thread tails from the machine-stitching on the quilt. Thread a hand needle with one or both of them and blindstitch the openings shut.

MAKING BIAS BINDING
(Alternate Binding Technique)

Bias binding takes longer to make than self-binding, but there are times you may prefer to use it, such as for a more finished look on an elegant or heirloom quilt or if you run short on self-binding fabric. Choose a binding fabric that coordinates with both the front and back of the quilt. This technique is more forgiving than double-fold bias or straight-of-grain binding; it will stretch or shrink to conform to the shape and width required, and it fits neatly around corners.

1 Position the fabric on the cutting mat as shown. Line up the 45-degree angle of the ruler with the lower selvedge and make one diagonal rotary cut.

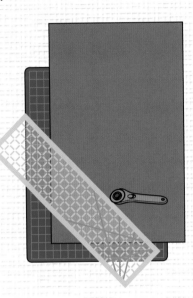

2 Fold the fabric, lining up the raw edges of the diagonal cut.

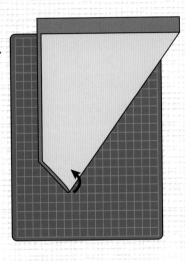

3 Mark the 2⅝" line of the ruler with transparent fluorescent tape or postable notes. Line up this 2⅝" line with the bias-cut, raw edge of the fabric, and rotary-cut a strip. Continue to cut additional strips. Depending on the size of your mat, the folded fabric may need to be repositioned one or more times. Trim the selvedges from the strips. Loosely place the strips around the perimeter of your quilt as you cut them so you can tell when you have enough. Be sure to allow extra for seams and turning corners.

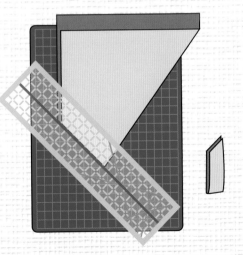

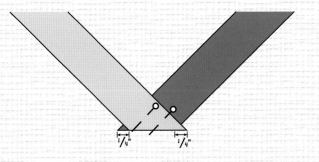

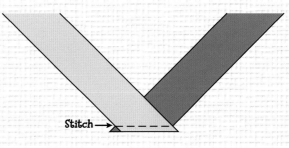

4 Pin two bias strips right sides together with ¼" triangle flaps extending out on each side.

5 Stitch the seam together with a ¼" seam allowance. Repeat with additional seams, making sure all seam allowances are positioned on the same side of the bias strip.

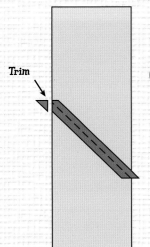

6 Gently press the seam open. Press along the grainline to avoid stretching the bias. Trim off overhanging triangles.

 TIP TO TRY

To keep finished bias binding from getting wrinkled before you sew it to your quilt, store it rolled around a toilet-paper or paper-towel tube.

ATTACHING BIAS BINDING

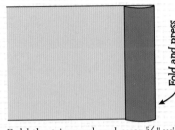

Trim bias strip end

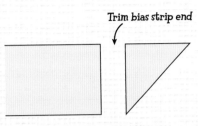

1 Trim one end of the bias strip to a right angle.

2 Fold the trimmed end over ⅝" with wrong sides together, and press.

Fold and press

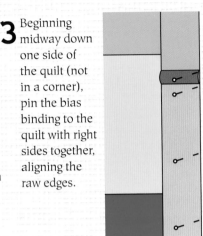

3 Beginning midway down one side of the quilt (not in a corner), pin the bias binding to the quilt with right sides together, aligning the raw edges.

⅝"

⅝"

4 Using a seam gauge to measure, mark a dot on the binding, ⅝" in from both sides of the corner of the quilt.

5 Stitch the pinned bias to the quilt using a ⅝" seam allowance, stopping at the dot. Backstitch at the corner and remove the pins.

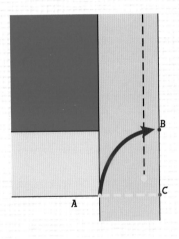

B

A   C

6 Pinch Point A between two fingers, lift it and bring it to Point B, folding up along the dotted line while holding Point C down so it doesn't shift. Pin.

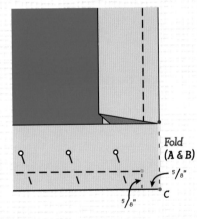

Fold (A & B)

⅝"

⅝"

C

7 Pin the bias along the rest of that side of the quilt. Measure and mark the dot. Beginning at the dot, stitch the bias binding to the quilt.

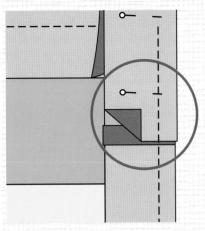
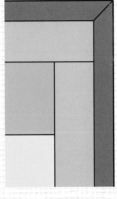

TIP TO TRY

In this method, the instructions direct you to stitch the binding to the quilt one side at a time. Once you have practiced this method and are familiar with how to fold the corners to avoid extra bulk, you may want to pin the bias around all four sides first, and then stitch them all at once.

8 Follow Steps 3–7 on the remaining sides. When you get to the beginning of the binding, overlap the fold and trim. (To allow for shifting while stitching, don't trim too closely.) Stitch and remove the pins.

9 Unfold the binding all around the quilt, opening the corners and pressing lightly from the right side if desired.

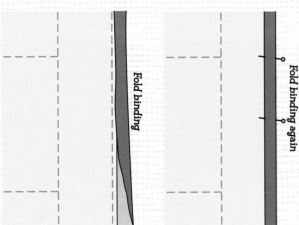

Fold binding

Fold binding again

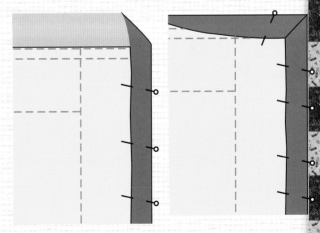

10 Place the quilt with the backing side up. On one side of the quilt, fold the binding in half, wrong sides together, so the raw-edge of the binding butts up to the raw-edge of the quilt. Fold again to just cover the ⅝" stitching line. Pin.

11 At the corner, the bias binding will naturally fold into a mitered corner. Handstitch the binding down to finish.

CHARITY AND COMMUNITY-SERVICE QUILTS
SPEEDING UP THE HEALING PROCESS WITH 90-MINUTE QUILTS

There are moments when the comfort of a special quilt is needed as soon as possible, and 90-Minute Quilt techniques can help. My daughter was a student at Virginia Tech at the time of the shootings in 2007, and I lived in California—too far away for hugs. So I dove into the next best thing: making her a quilt. I completed her HOKIE HOPE lap quilt just hours after receiving the VT collegiate fabrics in the mail, and she told me that as she opened the box she felt my hugs pour out.

I also used my basic 90-Minute methods to make a three hundred-piece Virginia Tech healing quilt for the university, titled HUGS FOR HOKIES: HEARTS AND HANDS REACH OUT TO VIRGINIA TECH. It features the Virginia Tech logo fabric in the center surrounded by hands reaching out in comfort. I embellished it with a sprinkling of hearts to represent the love being poured out to the school. Even though it is a complex quilt, it was completed in just a couple of days by using basic 90-Minute Quilt construction methods.

Barely two weeks after the shootings, both quilts were on exhibit at the Print Concepts booth at Quilt Market in Salt Lake City along with information for donating to the Hokie Spirit Memorial Fund.

These very special quilts were healing for me to make, for the recipients to receive and for the many people who have viewed them.

HUGS FOR HOKIES:
HEARTS AND HANDS REACH OUT
TO VIRGINIA TECH
(Photo courtesy of Theresa Locke)

Meryl Ann and the HOKIE HOPE lap quilt. Collegiate logo fabrics by Sykel.
(Photo courtesy of Theresa Locke)

The group quilts I coordinated for THE FIRST US-SOVIET CHILDREN'S PEACE QUILT EXCHANGE PROJECT (1987–1988) and NELSON MANDELA'S ANTI-APARTHEID: LOVE FOR ALL MANKIND QUILT PROJECT (1993) also used 90-Minute construction methods in order to complete the projects quickly. These quilts served to turn international attention toward a more balanced sense of global well-being.

THE FIRST US-SOVIET CHILDREN'S PEACE QUILT EXCHANGE was a citizen diplomacy project between a sixth grade class at Linkhorn Park Elementary School, Virginia Beach, Virginia, and School 119 in Odessa, Ukraine. Two quilts featured the children's drawings of peace on fabric. The schools swapped quilts in the first quilt exchange between the two countries.

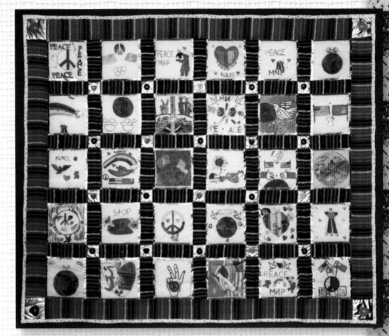

The American children's quilt
(Photo courtesy of Paul Varelas)

Meryl Ann, a former Girl Scout, coaches Troop 2286 from Newport, Virginia, in her 90-Minute Quilt techniques.
(Photo courtesy of Christy Porterfield)

In 2007, I started long-distance quilt coaching for a Girl Scout troop in Virginia, and they have stitched many dozens of quilts for Project Linus since then.

In 2010 their local Project Linus chapter requested quilts for the survivors of the Haitian earthquake, and needed them in two weeks. Luckily, the troop had several snow days off of school, and they completed twenty-two quilts by the deadline! Troop leader Christy Porterfield said, "The girls were so happy to help other children so far away with something that these children will likely hold closely while they are in transition."

CONSIDER THIS!

Project Linus and Quilts for Kids are both 501(c)3 non-profit organizations of volunteers that make and distribute charity quilts. Visit them at www.projectlinus.org and www.quiltsforkids.org.

Girl Scouts Alyssa and Victoria working on Cole's quilt.
(Photo courtesy of Christy Porterfield)

In 2008, magazine editor Beth Vitiritto's ten-year-old, sports-enthusiast nephew faced a sudden, critical illness. I mentioned it to the scouts who jumped into action for a boy they'd never met. They stitched Cole a cozy, all-flannel 90-Minute Quilt with his favorite sports motifs on it for him to snuggle in during chemotherapy.

The girls finished the quilt in time to celebrate Cole's eleventh birthday with an "across the miles" party in his honor! The girls included his favorite foods—pizza and Mountain Dew—and even made a birthday cake with a baseball and mitt on top. They included photos and some of the party decorations along with the quilt they shipped to Cole.

As long as life offers challenging moments, we quilters are lucky to be able to respond with stitches of love. After all, they don't call quilts "comforters" for nothing! And the faster we can finish these quilts, the sooner the recipients can envelop themselves in our gifts of comfort.

Cole is delighted at opening his "celebration in a box" from the Girl Scouts he'd never met.
(Photo courtesy of Beth Vitiritto)

The scouts celebrate Cole's birthday.
(Photo courtesy of Christy Porterfield)

VARIATION: QUICK CHARITY QUILT

Most of the quilts in this book are perfect for community service and charity quilt projects, particularly the basic 90-Minute Quilts such as SERENGETI RAINBOWS (page 48), SONGBIRD WHEELCHAIR QUILT (page 86) and MAGICAL MEADOWS (page 52). Once the squares are cut, it's possible to stitch up several in a day with these methods.

BEE HAPPY is a Project Linus quilt made using the basic instructions for SERENGETI RAINBOWS. It was long-arm quilted with a charming bumblebee design, but it could also be quilted in the same way as the quilts mentioned above.

FABRIC AND NOTIONS:

- ⅝ yd. happy sun and bumblebee fabric

- ⅜ yd. turquoise bumblebee fabric

- ⅝ yd. yellow-orange batik floral

- 1½ yds. golden yellow-orange flannel (backing/binding)

- Two packages of craft-sized cotton batting (used as a double layer for added loft)

- Coordinating thread for piecing and bobbin

- Variegated blue-green thread for long-arm quilting

- ½" wide Steam-A-Seam 2 fusible web tape

PREPARE AND CUT

- Prewash and trim the flannel to 51"/52" long

- Eleven 6" squares from the happy sun and bumblebee fabric

- Eight 6" squares from the turquoise bumblebee fabric

- Sixteen 6" squares from the yellow-orange batik floral

SEW

Lay out squares as shown and follow instructions for SERENGETI RAINBOWS, beginning with Step 1.

BEE HAPPY

Finished quilt: 30" × 41"
Pieced and bound by Carole Dull, long-arm quilted by Barbara Sheipe, fabrics and long-arm quilting donated by Sarah's Thimble Quilt Shoppe.

DESIGNING YOUR OWN LAYOUTS

To Use Design Pieces:

Method A

Photocopy as many of the design pieces at the bottom of this page as you like. Add your own designs or values to blank shapes with pen or pencil. Cover the back of the paper with repositionable glue. (This glue makes your paper act like a postable note, and is available at office supply stores.) Cut out the horizontal strips, and then cut individual squares as you need them. Apply the squares to a blank or lined piece of paper to develop your design, repositioning as needed. This works on a vertical or horizontal surface.

Method B

Photocopy the design pieces at the bottom of this page onto cardstock. Cut squares as desired, and use them like puzzle pieces to develop designs.

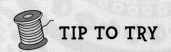

TIP TO TRY

Kids love designing quilts with these methods, too! Their paper designs can be their finished projects, and they'll learn about color and patterns in the process.

Design Pieces

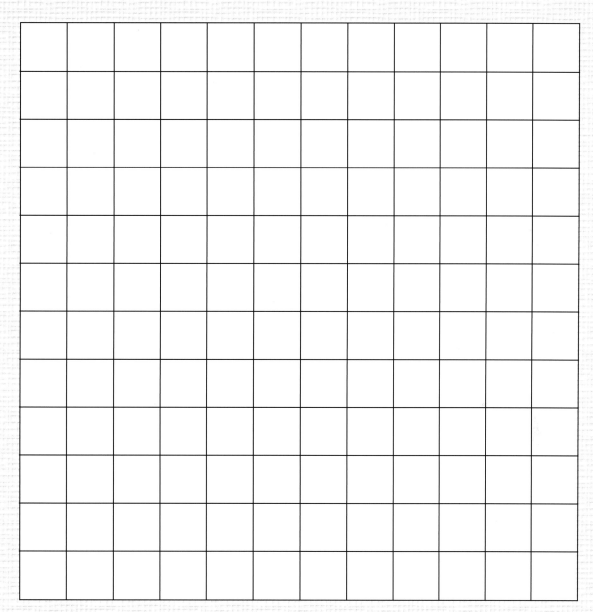

Universal Grid

Photocopy the appropriate portion of this grid to design a custom-sized 90-Minute Quilt with colored pencils.

PROJECTS

Welcome to some of the fastest and most fun quilts you'll ever make! Once you become familiar with the quick piecing and quilting methods shown here, you can stitch up a little 30" × 41" crib or preschooler-sized quilt in no time! Your first or even your second 90-Minute Quilt project will probably take more than an hour and a half because you will need time to learn and perfect the new techniques. But once you master the time-saving methods, you'll find you can finish these happy little quilts in about ninety minutes of stitching time, including piecing, quilting, binding and even a rod pocket for hanging.

SERENGETI RAINBOWS

I stitched SERENGETI RAINBOWS late one evening with just two small pieces of fabric from my stash, plus the backing. Bright and exciting fabrics do most of the work for you in this simple checkerboard layout.

Finished quilt: 30" × 41"
Sample stitched by the author

FABRIC AND NOTIONS:

- ⅝ yd. geometric multicolor (squares)
- ⅝ yd. gradated rainbow (squares)
- 1 ⅝ yds. yellow geometric flannel (backing/binding)
- Batting: Craft size (or about 36" × 48")
- Thread for piecing in neutral color
- Thread for bobbin to match backing
- Contrast thread for quilting
- ½" wide Steam-A-Seam 2 fusible web tape

In This Project:

Tapa Geometric by Alexander Henry and Puzzle Pieces by Moda; Flannel by Blank Quilting; Warm & Natural batting by the Warm Company

TOOLS AND SUPPLIES:

- Basic 90-Minute Quilt tools (see pages 8–13)
- 6" × 24" ruler

PREPARE

Prewash the flannel. Trim to 51" long. Prewash the other fabrics if desired.

CUT

- Eighteen 6" squares from the geometric multicolor fabric
- Seventeen 6" squares from the gradated rainbow fabric

LAYOUT

Arrange the squares on a flat design surface, referring to the layout quilt image on page 51 to create the look shown. Pin a postable note on the top square in each column, numbering them from left to right. Stack the squares in each column, being careful to keep them in order.

SEW

Note: All seam allowances are ¼" unless otherwise noted. If available, use a walking foot with a ¼" marking or use a ¼" quilting foot with an even-feed mechanism engaged. Both save time, prevent fabric slippage and minimize unwanted tucks.

1 Stitch the squares together in order in each column. This creates five columns with seven squares in each.

2 Press seam allowances up (toward the top square with the label) on even-numbered columns. Press seam allowances down on odd-numbered columns.

3 Place the flannel backing on a flat surface, right side down, and smooth out any wrinkles. Center the batting on top of the backing.

4 Pin Column 3 in the center of the batting. Sew all the columns down (see Sewing the Columns on pages 26–28). Check the stitching on the back of the quilt to make sure there are no unwanted tucks, and remove the postable notes.

QUILT

1 Pin all the raw edges of the squares through the batting/backing unit to stabilize them.

2 Quilt using contrasting top thread and bobbin thread to match the backing.

BIND

Trim the backing to 3½" and the batting to 1¼" and complete the self-binding (see Self-Binding on pages 32–35).

VARIATION

A basic 90-Minute variation of Serengeti Rainbows, this quilt uses sueded hand dyed gradation fabrics by Cherrywood.

In the collection of Cathy and Ed O'Neill, Los Angeles
(Photo courtesy of Meryl Ann Butler)

Layout Quilt

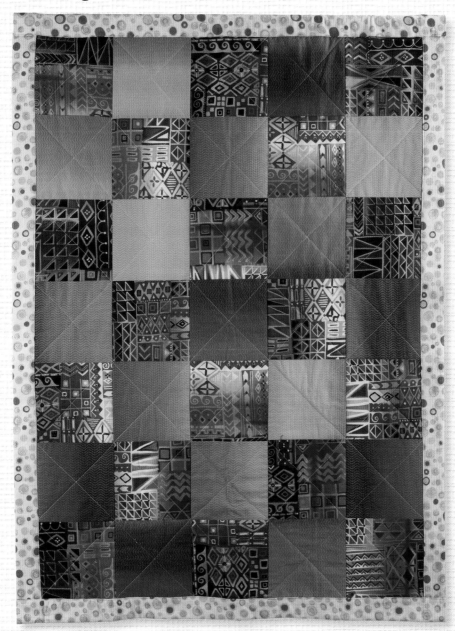

VARIATION: MAGICAL MEADOWS

FABRIC AND NOTIONS:

- ½ yd. of lilac multifloral print (fussy-cut for pieced center square) or sufficient yardage to cut four 3½" squares from exactly the same motif area
- ¼ yd. lime rickrack print (squares)
- ⅜ yd. apricot multfloral print (squares)
- ⅜ yd. lilac plaid butterfly print (squares)
- ⅜ yd. lime butterfly print (squares)
- ¼ yd. apricot tonal floral fabric (squares)
- 1⅝ yd. flannel (backing/binding)
- Batting: Crib size (or about 36" × 48")
- Thread for piecing in neutral color
- Thread for bobbin to match backing
- Contrast thread for quilting
- ½" wide Steam-A-Seam 2 fusible web tape

In This Project:

All fabrics for blocks by Me and My Sister for Moda; Moda Marbles flannel; Fairfield's Nature-Fil bamboo batting; Sulky Blendables thread color #4103 (Pansy)

PREPARE

Prewash the flannel. Trim to 51" long. Prewash other fabrics if desired.

CUT

- Fussy-cut four identical 3½" × 3½" squares from the lilac multicolor floral. (These are cut slightly larger than needed; the outside will be trimmed after stitching.)
- Four 6" squares from the lime rickrack fabric
- Eight 6" squares from the apricot multicolor floral fabric
- Ten 6" squares from the lilac butterfly fabric
- Eight 6" squares from the lime butterfly fabric
- Four 6" squares from the apricot tonal floral fabric

Finished quilt: 30" × 41"
Sample stitched by Cyndi Rudy

CREATE THE CENTER FOUR-PATCH

Arrange the set of four identical 3½" squares, positioning the same area of the design in the center of the Four-Patch. Follow the instructions on page 15 to create a 6" kaleidoscope center for your quilt.

Note: The overall look of the Four-Patch unit changes slightly after the seams are stitched.

SEW AND FINISH

Follow the steps for Layout, Sew, Quilt and Bind for SERENGETI RAINBOWS to complete your MAGICAL MEADOWS quilt.

VARIATION: GIVE 'EM SOMETHING TO TALK ABOUT

This conversation charm quilt will give any kid something to talk about! A "conversation" print is any fabric with images of items that inspire dialogue rather than nonobjective or floral patterns. A charm quilt is one in which each piece is the same geometric shape but is cut from a different fabric. You can make this version quickly with just thirty-five assorted, precut squares.

FABRIC AND NOTIONS:

- Thirty-five precut 6" squares
- Batting: Craft size (or about 36" × 45")
- 1 ⅝ yds. blue flannel (backing/binding)
- Thread for piecing in neutral color
- Thread for bobbin to match backing
- Multicolored thread for quilting

In This Project:

"Kid-Pleasing 6 Inch Print Collection" (charm pack of 60 assorted squares) from Keepsake Quilting; Back to Back's Pacafil alpaca/cotton blend batting; Animal Alphabet Dot Blue flannel by Cheri Strole for Moda; Sulky Blendables #4126 Primary Rainbow thread

Finished quilt: 30" × 41"
Sample stitched by Peggy Jebavy

LAYOUT

1 Identify the main color in each fabric square in the collection (which will vary from the squares shown) and sort the squares into piles of like colors. If you have trouble identifying the major color in a multicolor fabric, use this professional artist's trick: Squint your eyes to filter out "noise." This allows the predominant values and colors of each square to be more apparent.

2 Choose a center square. Arranging the squares on a flat design surface, work your design out from the center. Refer to the layout quilt image to create a look similar to that shown.

SEW AND FINISH

Follow the remaining steps for Layout, Sew, Quilt and Bind for SERENGETI RAINBOWS to complete your GIVE 'EM SOMETHING TO TALK ABOUT quilt.

SPRING PANSIES BOLSTER PILLOW

Decorate all year long with these charming pillows you can stitch up in about thirty minutes. Create a couple for each season to make any room festive in moments! Out-of-season bolster covers can be stored flat and used to recover the same pillow form as the seasons change. This "low-sew" project also makes a lovely bazaar item or gift.

Endless Summer Variation

Autumn Jack-O-Lantern Variation

Winter's Angel Variation

FABRIC AND NOTIONS:

- 5" × 14" bolster pillow form
- ¼ yd. pansy motif main-focus fabric (center strip)
- ⅛ yd. contrast light green crosshatched fabric (border strips)
- ½ yd. contrast fabric (self-ruffle)
- 13½" × 21" piece of muslin
- Batting: 13" × 20½" ultrathin low loft
- 2½ yds. of ⅝" wide coordinating Jacquard ribbon trim
- 2½ yds. of 1½"–2½" wide coordinating ribbon, cut into two 1¼ yd. pieces (ties)
- ¼" wide Steam-A-Seam 2 double-stick fusible web tape
- Thread for piecing in neutral color
- Thread for bobbin to match backing
- Contrasting purple thread for edgestitching

In This Project:
Pretty Face collection by Ro Gregg for Northcott; Pansy Jacquard ribbons by LFN Textiles; Thermore Ultrathin Batting by Hobbs; Soft Touch pillow form by Fairfield

TOOLS AND SUPPLIES:

- Basic 90-Minute Quilt tools (see pages 8–13)
- Two rubber bands

PREPARE

Prewash fabrics as desired.

CUT

- One 6½" × 21" strip from main-focus fabric (fussy-cut motifs)
- Two 2" × 21" strips from contrast fabric
- Two 18" × 21" strips (self-ruffle)

VARIATIONS

(SEW AS FOR Spring Pansies)

ENDLESS SUMMER BOLSTER PILLOW
- ¼ yd. lime and aqua batik main-focus fabric
- ⅛ yd. contrast aqua swirl batik
- ½ yd. contrast lime and aqua leaf print batik (self-ruffle)
- 1¼ yds. of 2½" wide aqua floral Jacquard ribbon trim
- 1¼ yds. of ⅝" wide lime and aqua brocade ribbon trim
- 2½ yds. of 2½" wide turquoise wire-edge ribbon (ties)

(In This Project: Fabrics from Bali Batiks by Hoffman; Jacquard ribbons by LFN Textiles)

AUTUMN JACK-O-LANTERN BOLSTER PILLOW
- One 8" × 21" strip from pumpkin fabric (center strip)
- Two 2" × 21" strips from contrast off-white, glow-in-the-dark fabric (border strips)
- Two 18" × 21" orange with black dots print (self-ruffle)
- 1¼ yds. of ⅝" wide black grosgrain ribbon
- 1¼ yds. of ½" wide orange gingham ribbon
- 1¼ yds. of ³⁄₁₆" wide orange grosgrain ribbon
- 1¼ yds. of ⅛" wide black satin ribbon
- 2½ yds. of 1½"–2½" wide black ribbon (ties)
- Glow-in-the-dark thread for topstitching

(In This Project: Glow-in-the-Dark fabrics from Michael Miller and Henry Glass; Glow-in-the-Dark Superior Thread)

WINTER'S ANGEL BOLSTER PILLOW
- ¼ yd. angel motif main-focus fabric (center strip)
- ⅛ yd. contrast holly toss fabric (border strips)
- ½ yd. contrast ornate stripe fabric (self-ruffle; more may be needed to match stripes)
- 1¼ yds. coordinating Jacquard ribbon trim #1
- 1¼ yds. coordinating Jacquard ribbon trim #2
- 2½ yds. of 1½"–2½" wide coordinating ribbon (ties)

(In This Project: Fabrics by Judy Hansen for Fabri-Quilt; Jacquard ribbons by LFN Textiles)

Sew

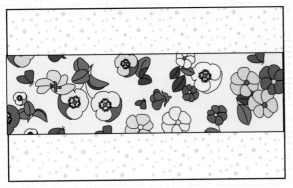

1 Place the muslin on a flat surface and center the batting on top. Pin the 6½" strip of focus fabric in the center of the muslin/batting unit. Measure to center it accurately.

2 Pin the two contrast strips to the focus fabric strip, right sides together, lining up raw edges. Be sure to pin through all layers.

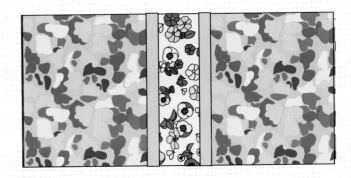

3 With ¼" seam allowance, stitch the strips together through the batting and the muslin. Open and press lightly.

4 Repeat with the contrast ruffle strips. (These will extend beyond the muslin/batting unit.)

 TIP TO TRY

If you can't find a ribbon in the color combo you need, stack a thinner ribbon on top of a wider ribbon. Baste in place with a gluestick or Steam-A-Seam 2 fusible web tape. Stitch stacked ribbons together with a straight or zigzag stitch. Apply to your pillow cover according to the project instructions.

5 Apply fusible web tape to the wrong side of the Jacquard ribbon trims with finger pressure, according to the manufacturer's instructions. (Or pin baste ribbons in place.) Place the ribbon trim over the seams, finger press to baste, and measure so the border strips look even. Adjust the ribbon as needed for the desired effect. Using a press cloth, fuse the ribbon in place with the iron set to a temperature that will not melt the ribbon (test on a scrap to be sure). Edgestitch or zigzag stitch on both sides of each ribbon using decorative thread if desired. Trim the excess ribbon.

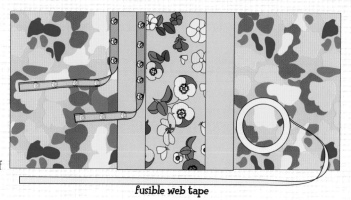

fusible web tape

6 Fold the stripped unit in half, lengthwise, right sides together, matching the placement of the ribbon trims. Pin. Stitch a long seam with ¼" seam allowance to form a tube.

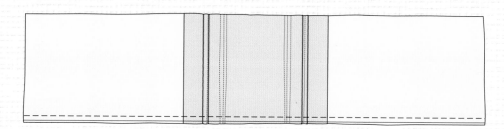

7 Turn the tube right side out. Place the bolster pillow inside, inserting the end with the tag on it first. Reach through the other side of the tube and pull the pillow into the middle of the cover by grasping the tag. It should fit snugly. Remove the pillow to adjust the seam allowance to fit, if necessary.

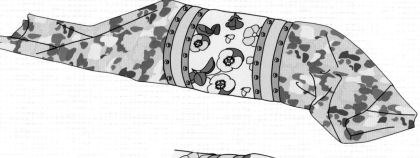

8 Fold the raw edges of both ends of the tube into the inside of the pillow cover to create a finished edge on the self-ruffle. Secure each side with a rubber band. Tie a satin or grosgrain ribbon in a bow to cover the rubber band. Trim the ribbon ties as needed.

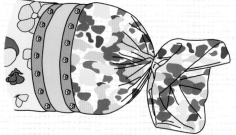

KITTYCORNER CATS

Cheerful cats romp diagonally across this snuggle-sized lap or crib quilt in a faux-rail-fence effect. Borders at the top and bottom add extra length, and the binding size is smaller on the sides to avoid the need for a pieced backing. As a nod to nocturnal feline fun, this project is quilted with glow-in-the-dark thread!

Finished quilt: 38½" × 65½"
Sample stitched by the author

FABRIC AND NOTIONS:

- 1 ⅝ yds. large border stripe cat motif fabric (or enough to cut fourteen 8" squares plus border strips)
- ¼ yd. black-with-white paw print (squares)
- ¼ yd. lime paw print (squares)
- ¼ yd. black with multiflower print (squares)
- ¼ yd. white with multiflower print (squares)
- ¼ yd. black with multitext print (squares)
- ¼ yd. white with multi-mini hearts (squares)
- Selected piece of panel print (or enough to cut an 8" center square)
- ¼ yd. pink paw print (border strip)
- 2¼ yds. flannel (backing/binding)
- Batting: Twin size (or about 42" x 70")
- Thread for piecing in neutral color
- Thread for bobbin to match backing
- Glow-in-the-dark contrast thread for quilting
- ¼" wide Steam-A-Seam 2 fusible web tape

In This Project:
Fabrics from Sue Marsh's Caterwauling collection by RJR Fabrics; Quilters Dream Orient Batting; NiteLite ExtraGlow glow-in-the-dark thread by Superior Threads

TOOLS AND SUPPLIES:

- Basic 90-Minute Quilt tools (see pages 8–13)
- 8" or 8½" square ruler
- 8½" × 24" ruler
- 90/14 topstitching or metallic machine needle (for glow-in-the-dark thread)

PREPARE

Prewash the flannel. Trim to 72" long. If the fabric shrinks to less than 41"/42" wide, piece the backing or plan to bind with bias. Prewash the other fabrics as desired.

CUT

- Fussy-cut two identical 8" wide strips along the border stripe; subcut these into fourteen 8" squares
- From the remainder of the border stripe fabric, cut two striped strips 3¼" × about 39" (inner border)
- Four 8" squares from the black-with-white paw print fabric (squares)
- Five 8" squares from the lime paw print fabric (squares)
- Two 8" squares from the black with multiflower print (squares)
- Two 8" squares from the white with multiflower print (squares)
- Two 8" squares from the black with multitext print (squares)
- Five 8" squares from the white with multi-mini hearts (squares)
- One 8" square from the selected panel print (center square)
- Two strips 2¾" wide from the pink paw print (outer border)

LAYOUT

Position the squares on a flat design surface, referring to the layout quilt image on page 61 to create the look shown.

SEW

1 Label and sew the squares together in order in each column. This creates five columns with seven squares in each. Press the seam allowances (up for even columns, down for odd columns).

2 Place the flannel backing on a flat surface, right side down, and center the batting on top. Mark the center of this batting/backing unit.

3 Line up the center of Column 3 with the marked center of the batting/backing unit. Measure from the edges of this column to center it as accurately as possible. This is especially important if your flannel is less than 42" wide. Pin in place.

4 Sew all the columns down (see Sewing the Columns on pages 26–28). Remove postable notes.

QUILT

Using glow-in-the-dark thread and a 90/14 topstitch needle, quilt in diagonal lines (see Quilting the Project on page 29) or as desired.

TIP TO TRY

The cut measurement of the inner striped border strip can be adjusted to accommodate specific stripes you wish to capture from your selected border print. Simply add or subtract that adjusted amount from the width that you will cut the outer border so the total width of the two cut pieces equals 6", and the size of the finished quilt will remain the same.

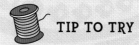

TIP TO TRY

When using NiteLite ExtraGlow thread, Bob Purcell, President of Superior Threads, recommends using a topstitch 90/14 needle and a top tension range of 3.0 to 3.5 for optimum performance and to avoid shredding.

BORDERS

1 Stitch the 3¼" inner striped borders to the top and bottom of the quilt. Trim flush with the raw edges of the pieced squares.

2 Stitch the 2¾" pink border to the top and bottom of the quilt. Trim flush with the raw edges of the pieced squares. Additional quilting may be added to the borders if desired.

BIND

1 On the top and bottom edges, trim the backing and the batting 3½" from the raw edges of the pink borders. Trim the BATTING ONLY 1¼" wide, measuring from the raw edges of the pink borders.

2 Trim the backing on the sides ONLY a generous 1". Carefully fold the backing under and trim the batting a scant ¼", measuring from the raw edges of the quilted squares. On the long sides, fold the backing over ¼", wrong sides together, and press. Fold again to cover the raw edges by ¼". Pin or use pressure sensitive fusible webbing tape to baste. Edgestitch.

3 Finish top and bottom of the self binding (see Self-Binding on pages 32–35).

QUILT OF MANY COLORS

What baby wouldn't love to be bundled up in his or her very own rainbow? This happy quilt is made from just eight strips of fabric! Each print has four coordinating stripes of color running the length of the goods, so each cut strip looks like it's already been pieced from four different values of the feature color.

Finished quilt: 30" × 41"
Sample stitched by Barbara Sheipe

FABRIC AND NOTIONS:

- ¼ yd. red fabric with lengthwise graded stripes
- ¼ yd. orange fabric with lengthwise graded stripes
- ¼ yd. green fabric with lengthwise graded stripes
- ¼ yd. teal-blue fabric with lengthwise graded stripes
- ¼ yd. royal-blue fabric with lengthwise graded stripes
- ¼ yd. purple fabric with lengthwise graded stripes
- ⅓ yd. yellow fabric with lengthwise graded stripes
- 2⅝ yd. flannel (backing/binding)
- Batting: Crib size (or about 42" × 55")
- Thread for piecing in neutral color
- Thread for bobbin to match backing
- Contrast thread for quilting
- ¼" wide Steam-A-Seam 2 fusible web tape

In This Project:
Twinkle fabrics by Yolanda Fundora for Blank Quilting; Tuscany crib-sized silk batting by Hobbs; Spring Girl Scouts flannel by Robert Kaufman; Sulky Blendables thread #4106

TOOLS AND SUPPLIES:

- Basic 90-Minute Quilt tools (see pages 8–13)
- 4½" × 24" ruler (or 6" × 24" ruler)

PREPARE

Prewash the flannel. Prewash the other fabrics as desired. Seam the flannel backing. Trim to 45" × 60".

CUT

- One strip, 4½" wide, selvedge to selvedge, from the red fabric
- One strip, 4½" wide, selvedge to selvedge, from the orange fabric
- One strip, 4½" wide, selvedge to selvedge, from the green fabric
- One strip, 4½" wide, selvedge to selvedge, from the teal fabric
- One strip, 4½" wide, selvedge to selvedge, from the blue fabric
- One strip, 4½" wide, selvedge to selvedge, from the purple fabric
- Two strips, 4½" wide, selvedge to selvedge, from the yellow fabric

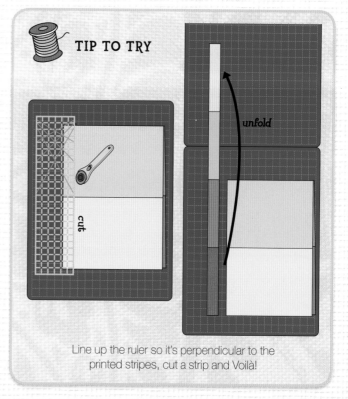

TIP TO TRY

unfold

cut

Line up the ruler so it's perpendicular to the printed stripes, cut a strip and Voilà!

LAYOUT

Arrange the strips on a flat design surface, referring to the layout quilt image on page 65 to create the look shown. Line up the center stripes horizontally, first. Then trim the ends of the strips as needed so they are all the same length. Pin a postable note to the top of each strip/column to number it.

SEW

1 Place the flannel backing on a flat surface, right side down, and center the batting on top. Mark the center of this batting/backing unit.

2 Line up the left-hand edge of Column 5 with the marked center of the batting/backing unit and pin in place.

3 Sew all the columns down (see Sewing the Columns on pages 26–28). Remove postable notes.

QUILT

1 Pin all the raw edges through the batting/backing unit to stabilize them.

2 Use contrasting top thread and bobbin thread to match the backing. Referring to the quilting diagrams below, start in any corner, backstitch first and then stitch diagonally across each rectangle. Backstitch at the end of the first pass. (Draw chalk guidelines first, if you like.)

3 Complete the second pass of quilting. Then, turn the quilt upside down and repeat the first and second passes. Continue to complete the third pass of quilting. Each rectangle will now have an X in it. Remove pins.

4 Staystitch around the perimeter within ¼" seam allowance.

BIND

Trim the backing to 3½" and the batting to 1¼" and complete the self-binding (see Self-Binding on pages 32–35).

Quilting Diagram

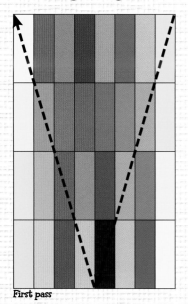

First pass

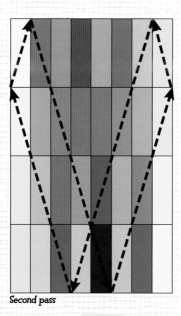

Second pass

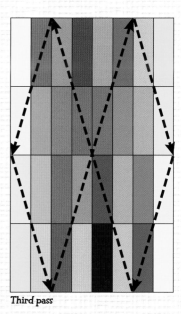

Third pass

LAYOUT QUILT

DANISH DELIGHT

A simple yet elegant Danish-design throw
with a classic Scandinavian look adds
a splash of subtle color to contemporary
interiors. This quilt only has twenty-six
pieces—the striped fabric does most of the
work for you!

Finished quilt: 44½" × 59"
Sample stitched by Peggy Jebavy

FABRIC AND NOTIONS:

- ⅞ yd. gray fabric with lengthwise graded stripes
- ⅞ yd. brown fabric with lengthwise graded stripes
- ⅛ yd. purple fabric with lengthwise graded stripes
- ⅛ yd. royal blue fabric with lengthwise graded stripes
- ⅛ yd. teal fabric with lengthwise graded stripes
- ⅛ yd. green fabric with lengthwise graded tripes
- ⅛ yd. yellow fabric with lengthwise graded stripes
- ⅛ yd. orange fabric with lengthwise graded stripes
- ⅛ yd. red fabric with lengthwise graded stripes
- ⅛ yd. pink fabric with lengthwise graded stripes
- 3¼ yds. flannel (backing/binding)
- Batting: Ultrathin twin size (or about 53" × 67")
- Thread for piecing in neutral color
- Thread for bobbin to match backing
- Contrast thread for quilting
- ¼" wide Steam-A-Seam 2 fusible web tape

In This Project:
Twinkle fabrics by Yolanda Fundora for Blank Quilting; Hey Cowboy flannel by RJR; Thermore batting by Hobbs; Sulky #4117 for contrast topstitching/quilting

TOOLS AND SUPPLIES:

- Basic 90-Minute Quilt tools (see pages 8–13)
- 6" × 24" ruler

PREPARE

Prewash the flannel. Prewash the other fabrics as desired. Make the flannel backing 55" × 69".

CUT

- Eight 3" strips from the gray fabric
- Eight 3" strips from the brown fabric
- One 2" strip from each of the remaining eight colors

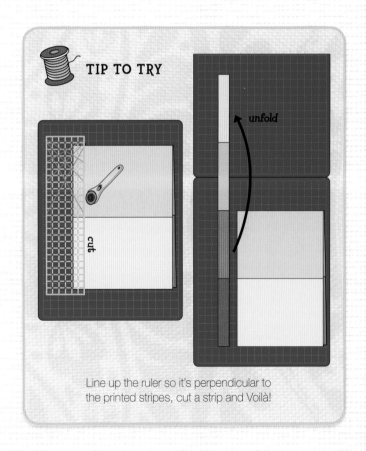

TIP TO TRY

unfold

cut

Line up the ruler so it's perpendicular to the printed stripes, cut a strip and Voilà!

Quilting Diagram

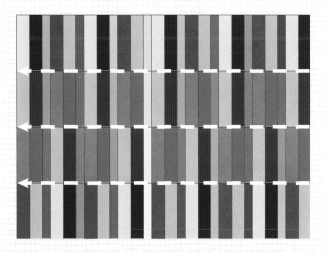

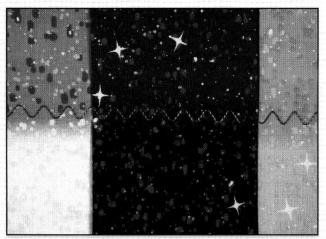

LAYOUT

1 Arrange the strips vertically on a flat design surface, referring to the layout quilt image on page 69 to create the look shown. Line up the horizontal color divisions. Trim ends to even up the strips as needed.

2 Number the strips (columns) 1–26.

SEW

1 Place the flannel backing on a flat surface, right side down, and center the batting on top. Mark the center of this batting/backing unit.

2 Line up the left edge of Column 14 with the marked center of the batting/backing unit, and pin in place.

3 Sew all the columns down (see Sewing the Columns on pages 26–28). Remove postable notes.

QUILT

Quilt your project using contrasting top thread and bobbin thread to match the backing (see Quilting the Project on page 29). Using the quilting diagram as a guide, faux stitch in the ditch with a simple decorative stitch across three horizontal "faux seams" where the colors in the strips change. (Draw chalk guidelines first, if you like.)

BIND

Trim the backing to 3½" and the batting to 1¼" and complete the self-binding (see Self-Binding on pages 32–35).

FENG SHUI GOOD LUCK

Kanji characters, such as the one in the center of this wall hanging, are Chinese characters used in the modern Japanese writing system. Kanji fabric squares typically come in a set and include motifs such as love, luck, success, longevity, faith, peace and prosperity. The quilt shown below centers around the kanji character for "good luck." Choose the sentiment you prefer and embellish your wall hanging with Chinese coins and a red tassel for even more good fortune!

Finished quilt: 29" × 29"
Sample stitched by Mary Menzer

FABRIC AND NOTIONS:

- ¼ yd. black tonal Asian print (squares)
- ¼ yd. bright red ginkgo-leaf print (half-square triangle units)
- ⅜ yd. gold-ochre/red-leaf print (half-square triangle units, 1st inner-frame border)
- ½ yd. black tonal Asian print (inner border, prairie point)
- ½ yd. red kanji print (middle border, prairie point)
- ½ yd. maroon ginkgo-leaf print (outer border)
- One 6" kanji-square fabric (center square)
- One scrap red Asian print large enough to cut a rectangle 8½" × 16"
- 1¼ yd. flannel (binding/backing)
- Batting: Craft size (or about 36" × 36")
- Thread for piecing in neutral color
- Thread for bobbin to match backing
- Contrast thread for quilting (red, metallic optional)
- Two small and one large gold-color beads
- One red tassel
- Four gold Chinese coin buttons
- Four small red fabric flowers (slightly larger than the buttons)
- One small red ribbon bow
- ¼" wide Steam-A-Seam 2 fusible web tape

In This Project:

Kanji square by Indonesian Batiks; fabrics by Kona Bay; Warm & Natural batting by the Warm Company; black flannel by RJR; Sulky Sliver gold #8003; Aurifil thread #2250 (red) and #2692 (black); Chinese coin buttons from buttondrawer.com; tassel by Wrights

TOOLS AND SUPPLIES:

- Basic 90-Minute Quilt tools (see pages 8–13)
- 5½" square ruler
- 6½" square ruler
- 6" × 24" ruler

PREPARE

Prewash and dry the flannel. Trim the flannel backing to 39" × 39".

CUT

- Four 5½" squares from the black tonal Asian print
- One 7¾" x 16" rectangle from the black tonal Asian print
- Two 6½" squares from the red ginkgo print (half-square triangle units)
- Two 6½" squares from the gold-ochre/red-leaf print (half-square triangle units)
- Two strips 1½" wide from the gold-ochre/red-leaf print; cut each strip in half
- Two strips 1¾" wide from the red kanji print; cut each strip in half
- One rectangle 8½" x 16" from the red kanji print
- Two strips 1⅛" wide from the black tonal print; cut each strip in half
- Three strips 3" wide from the maroon ginkgo print
- Trim the kanji square to 5½" square

Make Half-Square Triangle Units

1 Follow the instructions for Method #1 on page 17 to make the half-square triangle units. With a chalk marker, draw a diagonal line from corner to corner on the wrong side of the red squares. Stack them on top of the gold print squares with the right sides together.

2 With ¼" seam allowance, sew a line of stitching on both sides of the chalk line. Chain-sew for speed.

3 Rotary-cut along the chalk line.

4 Press the half-square triangles open with the seam allowance toward the darker fabric. Place a stitched square on a rotating mat, right side up. Place the 5½" square ruler on top of the square, lining up the 45-degree marking on the ruler with the stitched seam. Trim to a perfect 5½" square.

Layout

Position the squares and half-square triangle units on a flat design surface, referring to the layout quilt image on page 75 to create the look shown.

Sew

1 Label and sew the squares together in order in each column. Press the seam allowances (up for even columns, down for odd columns).

2 Place the flannel backing on a flat surface, right side down, and center the batting on top. Mark the center of this batting/backing unit.

3 Line up the center of Column 2 with the marked center of the batting/backing unit and pin in place.

4 Sew down Columns 1 and 3 (see Sewing the Columns on pages 26–28). Remove postable notes.

Quilt

1 Pin all the raw edges of the squares through the batting/backing unit to stabilize them.

2 Use contrasting top thread and bobbin thread to match the backing. Using the quilting diagrams shown below, start in the upper right corner, backstitch first and then stitch diagonally across that square, corner to corner, as shown. Then stitch in the ditch around the center block. Cover any red threads that have strayed onto black fabric with black permanent marker. Backstitch or tie the threads at the end of the first pass. Stitch short diagonals on the remaining three corner blocks.

3 Stitch diagonally across the black squares and in the ditch on the red and gold half-square triangle units as shown. Stitch only to within ¼" of the raw edges when pivoting.

Quilting Diagram

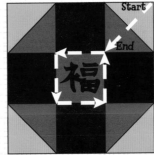

First Pass

Second Pass

Third Pass

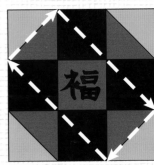

Fourth Pass

Borders

1 Stitch two gold print inner frame border strips to the sides, courthouse-steps style (see Adding Borders on pages 30 and 31). Then add the two gold print inner frame border strips to the top and bottom.

2 Repeat with the two black tonal inner border strips.

3 Repeat with the red kanji middle border strips.

4 Cut one of the maroon print outer border strips in half, and add these strips courthouse-steps style to the sides. Add the remaining strips to the top and bottom.

5 *Optional:* With metallic gold thread, stitch an outline on the maroon print outer border strips, approximately ¼" from the seam allowance and inside the borders of the kanji square.

Self-Binding

Trim the backing to 2¾" and the batting to 1" and complete the self-binding (see Self-Binding on pages 32–35).

Add embellishments

1 Add the piped prairie point to the bottom of the quilt (see instructions on page 74).

2 Stack the Chinese coin buttons on top of the red fabric flowers and handstitch them to the centers of the four black squares as shown in the layout quilt image on page 75.

3 Handstitch a red fabric bow to the top center of the prairie point as shown in the layout quilt image.

4 Thread the gold beads through the loop on top of the tassel and handstitch the tassel to the back of the point of the prairie point.

Optional outline quilting
stitches on center square

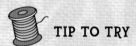 TIP TO TRY

If decorative buttons are too bright and shiny, simply antique them. Leave the buttons attached to the button card (for ease in handling). Brush a layer of black or brown acrylic paint onto the button and polish the wet paint off the "peaks" with a paper towel or cotton swab, letting the dark paint stay in the "valleys." Allow the buttons to dry before handstitching them to the quilt.

TIP TO TRY: MAKE THE PIPED PRAIRIE POINT

1 Stitch the red kanji print and black tonal rectangles together along the long edge.

2 Fold the unit wrong sides together, allowing ¼" of the red fabric to show on the black side, and press.

Fold

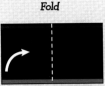

3 Fold the unit in half again with the right sides of the red fabric together. Press to mark the center.

Fold

4 Open the last fold. Fold both sides in so the bottom edges meet at the center fold.

Fold back

5 Draw a chalk line 2½" from each side of center and fold the sides back along these markings. Press.

Staystitch

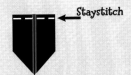

6 Staystitch ¼" from the top of the folded unit.

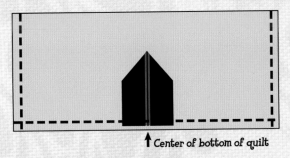

↑ Center of bottom of quilt

7 Line up the staystitching on the prairie point with the stitching on the back of the quilt. Pin the point in place. From the front, sew along the stitching line to attach the prairie point to the quilt.

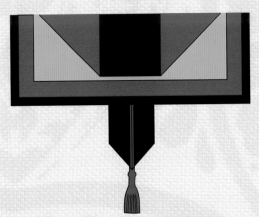

8 Flip the prairie point down and handstitch to secure it to the quilt. Add the tassel.

LAYOUT QUILT

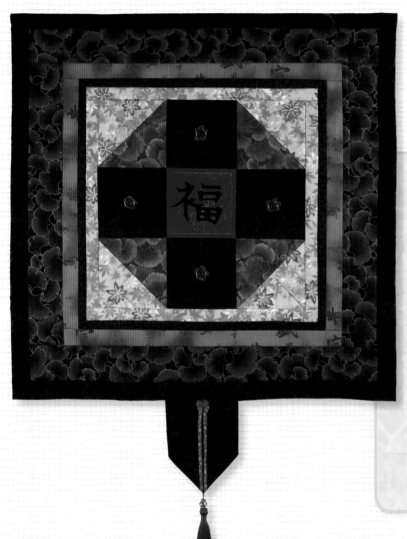

MAKE IT GREEN FOR BABY!

Using organic, ecofriendly fabrics and natural notions will start baby on the path to a green future. And you'll delight environmentally conscious moms, too! This summer-weight quilt has no batting—the heavy organic cotton flannel backing feels oh-so-velvety and provides just a touch of loft.

Finished quilt: 39½" × 51½"
Sample stitched by Deborah Renfrow

FABRIC AND NOTIONS:

- ½ yd. tan organic cotton gingham fabric 55" wide (squares, half-square triangle units)
- ¾ yd. blue organic wide-width (60" wide) cotton with words (fussy-cut squares)
- ¼ yd. teal organic cotton floral fabric 110" wide (squares)
- ¼ yd. soft white organic cotton 110" wide (squares, border)
- ½ yd. powder blue 110" wide organic cotton sateen (half-square triangle units, bias binding)
- ¼ yd. pale aqua 110" wide organic cotton sateen (border)
- 1 ⅜ yd. heavy organic flannel 54" wide (backing)
- Organic cotton thread for piecing and quilting

In This Project:

All by NearSea Naturals: Fabrics include Stumps Speak, Silent Stumps, Powder Blue, Whispering Grass, Pale Aqua, Soft White and Rich Brown Gingham Check; organic cotton Natural Heavy Flannel for backing; organic multipurpose thread

TOOLS AND SUPPLIES:

- Basic 90-Minute Quilt tools (see pages 8–13)
- 6½" × 24" ruler
- 6½" square ruler with diagonal center markings

> Note: You can make this quilt with standard width fabrics—just purchase additional yardage.

PREPARE

Prewash and dry the flannel in a natural, biodegradable, hypoallergenic laundry concentrate.

CUT

- Two 7½" squares and eight 6½" squares from the tan gingham fabric
- Eleven 6½" squares from the blue-with-words fabric
- Eight 6½" squares and two 7½" squares from the teal floral fabric
- Two 1½" × 34" strips, two 1½" × 44" strips and two 7½" squares from the soft white fabric
- Piece five yds. of bias strips 2⅝" wide from the powder blue fabric
- Two 7½" squares from the powder blue fabric
- Two 3¾" × 46" strips from the pale aqua solid fabric (outer side borders)
- Two 3¾" × 41" strips from the pale aqua solid fabric (outer top/bottom borders)

Make Half-Square Triangle Units

1 Pair up the 7½" squares, right sides together:
- White solid with teal floral (two sets)
- Tan gingham with blue solid (two sets)

2 Make the half-square triangles following Method #1 on page 17.

3 Place a stitched square on a rotating mat, right side up. Place the 6½" square ruler on top of the square, lining up the 45-degree marking on the ruler with the stitched seam. Trim to a perfect 6½" square.

TIP TO TRY

For a fast receiving blanket or throw for the nursery, just bind, serge or hem the edges of a heavyweight, coordinating organic fabric with a soft drape, like this cotton check by Michael Miller.

Sample stitched by Barbara Sheipe

Layout

Arrange the squares and half-square triangle units on a flat design surface, referring to the layout quilt image on page 79 to create the look shown.

Sew

1 Label and sew the squares together in order in each column. Press the seam allowances (up for even columns, down for odd columns).

2 Place the flannel backing on a flat surface, right side down, smoothing out any wrinkles. This quilt does not use batting. Mark the center of the backing.

3 Line up the center of Column 3 with the marked center of the backing, and pin.

4 Sew all the columns down (see Sewing the Columns on pages 26–28). Remove postable notes.

Quilt

Quilt your project using contrasting top thread and bobbin thread to match the backing (see Quilting the Project on page 29). Quilt as desired.

Borders

Add inner-white and outer-solid medium-teal borders, courthouse-steps style (see Adding Borders on pages 30 and 31). Quilt an outline along the seam line if desired. Staystitch edges if desired. Trim.

Bias Binding

Add bias binding to the edges of your quilt (see Making/Attaching Bias Binding on pages 36–39).

SWEET SCOTTIE

Stitch up this sweet Scottish terrier for
a darling baby quilt or wall hanging.
Her bow and tail are three-dimensional
half-square triangle units, and she bats
lovely embroidered eyelashes. Great Scott!
You can even make a reversed version with
a white doggy on a dark background!

Finished quilt: 39" × 30"
Sample stitched by Robin Fenn
and Barbara Sheipe

FABRIC AND NOTIONS:

- Fat ⅛ yd. or scraps of pink tonal prints (bow)
- Fat ⅛ yd. or scraps of eight to ten assorted white with black mini prints (background)
- Fat ⅛ yd. or scraps of six to eight assorted black tonal fabrics (dog)
- Fat ⅛ yd. or scraps of midvalue black-and-white prints (ground)
- 1½ yds. pink flannel (backing/binding)
- Batting: Craft size (or about 40" × 31")
- Thread for piecing in neutral color
- Thread for bobbin to match backing
- Light gray thread for quilting
- White thread for appliqué
- One skein bright pink embroidery floss
- Steam-a-Seam 2 pressure-sensitive fusible web tape
- Steam-a-Seam 2 pressure-sensitive fusible web scrap

In This Project:
All fabrics and flannel by P&B Textiles; Nature-Fil Bamboo batting by Fairfield; 40 wt. Aurifil thread #2600 gray and #3660 pink

TOOLS AND SUPPLIES:

- Basic 90-Minute Quilt tools (see pages 8–13)
- 6" × 24" ruler
- 5" square ruler
- 6" square ruler
- Press cloth

PREPARE

Prewash and dry the backing/binding flannel. Trim it to 41" × 46". Prewash the other fabrics as desired.

CUT

- Two 5" squares from the pink tonal prints
- Twenty-eight 5" squares from the assorted white-with-black mini prints (background)
- Two 6" squares from the two different white-with-black mini prints
- Two 6" squares from the two different black tonal prints
- Six 5" × 2¾" rectangles from the white-with-black mini prints
- Two 5" × 2¾" rectangles from the black tonal prints
- Eight 5" × 2¾" rectangles from the midvalue black-and-white overall print
- Eleven 5" squares from the assorted black tonal prints

Upper bow (make 1)   *Lower bow (make 1)*

Tail (make 1)

VARIATION

Robin Fenn, who quilted this sample, is planning to make a dachshund by adding another column or two to elongate the body of the dog!

MAKE HALF-SQUARE TRIANGLE UNITS

1 Pair up the two black tonal with the two white-with-black 6" squares and make half-square triangle units for a total of four (dog's face and ear) using Method #1 on page 17. Square the finished units to 5".

2 Press two pink 5" squares and one black tonal 5" square in half, diagonally, wrong sides together, pressing carefully to avoid stretching. Spray with water while pressing to form a flat, crisp fold.

3 Pair one pink pressed triangle with a white-with-black mini print square, and pin (upper bow).

4 Pair one pink pressed triangle with a white-and-black half-square triangle unit, and pin, using the image at left as a guide (lower bow).

5 Pair the black tonal pressed triangle with a white-with-black mini print square, and pin (tail).

MAKE APPLIQUÉ EYE

1 Choose one black tonal square for the main square of Sweet Scottie's head.

2 Select an appropriate section of black-and-white floral fabric for the eye. Adhere the scrap of fusible web to the wrong side of the fabric according to the manufacturer's directions.

3 Draw a circle on the remaining release paper using a dollar coin or other 1"–1⅛" diameter circle as a template. Line up the circle with the area of the print you have selected for the eye. Cut out. Remove the backing paper and adhere the eye circle to roughly the center of the black square using finger pressure. (Moving the eye slightly off center gives a bit more personality!) Satin stitch around the eye with white thread. Use a black permanent marking pen to tame any unruly stitches. (For a wall hanging, a button may be used, but appliqué is safer for a baby quilt.)

Layout

Position the squares and rectangles on a flat design surface, referring to the layout quilt image on page 85 to create the look shown.

Sew

1 Label and stitch the squares together in order in each column, being careful to preserve the orientation of the folded triangles and half-square triangle units for the ear, face and tail. Folded triangles will be caught in seams. This creates eight columns.

2 Press seam allowances up (toward the top square with the label) on even-numbered columns and press seam allowances down on odd-numbered columns with this exception: on the fourth square down from the top in Column 7 (muzzle), press the seam allowance toward the lighter fabric. Trim any dark fabric that shows through.

3 Place the flannel backing on a flat surface, right side down, smoothing out any wrinkles. Center the batting on top of the backing. Mark the center with a pin.

4 Line up the left-hand edge of Column 5 with the marked center of the batting/backing unit, and pin in place.

5 Sew all the columns down (see Sewing the Columns on pages 26–28). Remove postable notes.

Quilt

Use light gray top thread and bobbin thread to match the backing. Stitch in the ditch across all horizontal seams. Use a black permanent marking pen to color in any stray gray stitches on the black fabrics.

Bind

Trim the backing to 3½" and the batting to 1¼" and complete the self-binding (see Self-Binding on pages 32–35).

Finish

1 Tie the quilt with pink embroidery floss: Cut the floss about 13" long, thread the needle and double the thread. With a chalk marker, mark the centers of the squares you will tie.

2 Insert the needle and bring it through to the front.

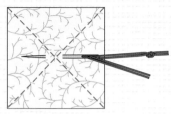

3 Cut the threads to remove the needle.

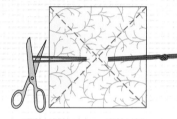

4 Tie a double knot.

5 Trim the tails to 1" long. Add additional ties for the nose if desired. Using 3 or 4 strands of floss, stitch on 4 eyelashes.

VARIATION: GREAT SCOTT!

GREAT SCOTT! was made by Carole Dull for a dog lover. She used nine different white-with-black mini prints for the Scottie and seventeen different black-with-white mini prints in the background. One of the background prints features a starry sky with constellations—including Canis Minor, one of Orion's dogs. Carole used a variety of six different middle-value prints for the ground, one of which had circles just perfect for fussy-cutting an eye. A red, white and black plaid bow tie dresses him right up!

Carole quilted this using the standard 90-Minute Quilt diagonal quilting pattern. When she got to the three-dimensional half-square triangle units, she simply lifted them up and stitched under them as far as she could for a finished look. On the bottom row, Carole made sure the center of her X's lined up with the horizontal seam.

Make both Scotties as separate quilts and hang them facing each other for a canine yin and yang!

Sample stitched by Carole Dull
In This Project: Fabrics from Half Moon by Moda and and Pen and Ink by P&B Textiles

SONGBIRD WHEELCHAIR QUILT

The flannel squares of this quilt feel soft and comforting to sensitive hands. The silk noil backing has a drape that hugs the body, and its nubby texture keeps it from slipping. The relatively light weight of this wheelchair quilt can be beneficial for people suffering from circulation issues or arthritis, while the silk noil provides a sense of cozy comfort. And believe it or not, silk noil is as easy to stitch as a midweight cotton!

Finished quilt: 33" × 35"
Sample stitched by Carole Dull

FABRIC AND NOTIONS:

- ½ yd. rose and green diagonal stripe flannel (squares)
- ½ yd. yellow/orange diagonal stripe flannel (squares)
- ⅜ yd. rose songbird print flannel (rectangles)
- ⅜ yd. yellow songbird print flannel (rectangles)
- ½ yd. white with flower print flannel
- 1¼ yd. silk noil (backing/binding)
- Thread for piecing in neutral color
- Thread for bobbin to match backing
- Contrast thread for quilting
- ¼" wide Steam-a-Seam 2 fusible web tape

In This Project:
Flannels for squares and borders by Riley Blake; silk noil #623 Shrimp by Thai Silks; Shaklee Get Clean Fresh Laundry Concentrate (used for prewashing since it is gentle for sensitive skin)

Note: This project uses diagonal striped fabric in two colorways for a pronounced, 3-D effect. However, one colorway may be used. Simply use more yardage and cut out twenty-four identical squares.

TOOLS AND SUPPLIES:

- Basic 90-Minute Quilt tools (see pages 8–13)
- 6" × 24" ruler
- 5½" square ruler with diagonal center markings (for accurate fussy-cutting)

PREPARE

Prewash all fabrics in a laundry concentrate appropriate for sensitive skin. Dry the noil in a dryer (remove promptly) to preshrink. Noil may need to be prewashed twice as it may continue to shrink significantly the second time it is washed and dried.

CUT

- Twelve 5½" squares from the rose and green stripe (to fussy-cut, line up the diagonal line on the ruler with a selected stripe; I selected the lime green skinny stripe)
- Twelve 5½" squares from the yellow/orange stripe (line up the diagonal line on the ruler with the colored stripe that corresponds to the stripe selected in the previous colorway; in this fabric it is the yellow skinny stripe)
- Nine 3" × 5½" rectangles from the rose songbird background flannel (fussy-cut three birds facing left, two birds facing right and four random floral)
- Nine 3" × 5½" rectangles from the yellow songbird background flannel (fussy-cut three birds facing left, two birds facing right and four random floral)
- Four 2¾" wide strips from the white with multiflower print flannel (fussy-cut if desired)

LAYOUT

Arrange the squares and rectangles on a flat design surface, referring to the layout quilt image on page 89 to create the look shown.

> Note: The songbird motifs on both the top and bottom of the quilt are arranged so they will be upright when the quilt is on the recipient's lap no matter which way the quilt is turned.

SEW

1 Label and sew the squares and rectangles together in order in each column. This creates six columns with seven rectangles and squares in each. Press seam allowances (up for even columns, down for odd columns).

2 Mark the center of the noil backing by pressing lightly. Place the backing on a flat surface, right side down, smoothing out any wrinkles.

3 Line up the left-hand edge of Column 4 with the marked center of the backing and pin in place.

4 Sew all the columns down (see Sewing the Columns on pages 26–28). Remove postable notes.

🧵 TIP TO TRY

Sizes of wheelchair quilts might vary from 24" × 32" to 36" × 48", depending on the size of both the wheelchair and the recipient. Measure so the quilt won't get caught in the wheels. This quilt can be made smaller or larger simply by adjusting the size of the squares used. You can also attach ribbon ties or Velcro loops 8"–10" from the top of the quilt to tie the quilt to the wheelchair.

QUILT

Quilt your project using contrasting top thread and bobbin thread to match the backing (see Quilting the Project on page 29). Quilt as desired or as shown below.

BORDERS

Add borders, log-cabin style (see Adding Borders on pages 30 and 31).

BIND

Trim the noil backing to 1¼" and complete the self-binding (see Self-Binding on pages 32–35).

Quilting Diagram

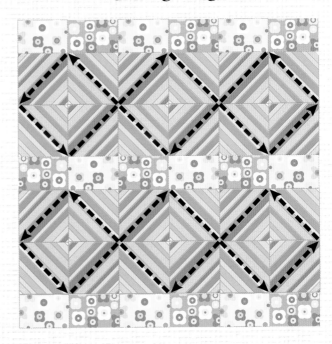

Layout Quilt

SUMMER-OF-LOVE
FLOOR PILLOW

Funky peace-and-love fabrics season this
24" floor pillow with retro flavor, and a
clever no-sew closure makes it easy to
stitch up. Just pop in a pillow form and hang
loose while you groove to the oldies. Can
you dig it?

Finished quilt: 22½" × 22½"
Sample stitched by Robin Fenn

FABRIC AND NOTIONS:

- Fat ⅛ or ¼ yd. large pink and orange on brown floral (pinwheel squares)
- Fat ⅛ or ¼ yd. pink and avocado swirl (pinwheel squares)
- Fat ⅛ or ¼ yd. red peace-doodles print (background)
- Fat ⅛ or ¼ yd. brown peace-doodles print (background)
- Fat ⅛ or ¼ yd. peace-signs print (background)
- Fat ⅛ or ¼ yd. peace-words print (background)
- Fat ⅛ or ¼ yd. small dark brown print (pinwheel triangles)
- Fat ⅛ or ¼ yd. butterflies print (background)
- Fat ⅛ or ¼ yd. mini pink and orange floral (pinwheel triangles)
- ¼ yd. brown/green/pink/orange stripe (inner border)
- 1¾ yd. brown peace-sign with flowers print (outer border, backing)
- 27" × 27" piece of flannel (any color—will not be seen)
- Batting: Craft size (or about 26" × 26")
- 24" firm pillow form (or larger squishy one)
- Thread for piecing in neutral color
- Thread for bobbin to match backing
- Contrast thread for quilting

In This Project:

Fabrics by Michael Miller; Back to Back's alpaca/cotton blend batting; Sulky Blendables thread # 4126

Note: Choose coordinating fabrics with peace motifs and a retro look to give this project its vintage 1960s charm.

TOOLS AND SUPPLIES:

- Basic 90-Minute Quilt tools (see pages 8–13)
- 5½" × 24" ruler
- 4½" and 5½" square rulers

PREPARE

Prewash the flannel. Prewash the other fabrics as desired.

CUT

- Two 4½" squares from the large pink and orange floral on brown (fussy-cut if desired)
- Two 4½" squares from the pink and avocado swirl
- Two 4½" squares from the red peace-doodles print
- Two 4½" squares from the brown peace-doodles print
- Two 4½" squares from the peace-signs print
- Two 4½" squares from the peace-words print
- One 5½" square from the small dark brown print
- Two 5½" squares from the butterflies print
- One 5½" square from the mini pink and orange floral
- Four strips 1½" wide from the brown/green/pink/orange stripe
- Four strips 3½" wide and two 23" × 28" rectangles from the brown peace-sign with flowers print

MAKE HALF-SQUARE TRIANGLE UNITS

1 Pair up the 5½" square of the retro-look small pink and orange print with a 5½" square of retro-look butterflies print.

2 Pair up the 5½" square of the retro-look small dark brown print with a 5½" square of retro-look butterflies print.

3 Make half-square triangle units (see page 17). Trim to 4½" square.

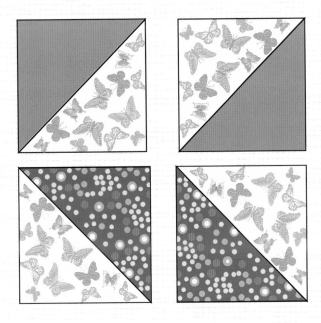

LAYOUT

Position the squares on a flat design surface, referring to the layout quilt image on page 95 to create the look shown.

TIP TO TRY

If the colors in one fabric seem too light and bright to coordinate with the other fabrics, you can dull the colors and slightly darken the values by overdyeing the fabric in tea or coffee. In this case, the design of the lime and pink fabric was just right for a 1960s theme, but the colors were just a little too bright and light, and the stark white didn't coordinate with the off-whites in the other fabrics. A tan overdye solved all the problems: It dulled and slightly darkened the lime and bright pink into avocado and rose and turned the bright white into off-white.

To overdye:
Cut a piece of fabric about an inch larger all around than the final size needed. (For this project I cut a piece about 6" × 10".) Wash and dry if not prewashed. Make strong coffee or tea in a glass or ceramic container large enough to accommodate your piece of fabric. Dip the fabric in the hot liquid and swish it around with a spoon for thirty to ninety seconds or more. Remove, rinse with cool water, press between towels or paper towels and iron dry. If it's not dark enough, repeat the process. Cut dyed fabric piece into the finished size(s) needed.

Sew

1 Label and sew the squares into columns. This creates four columns with four squares in each. Press seam allowances (up for even columns, down for odd columns).

2 Place the flannel backing on a flat surface, right side down, and center the batting on top. Mark the center of this batting/backing unit.

3 Line up the left-hand edge of Column 3 with the marked center of the batting/backing unit, and pin in place.

4 Sew all the columns down (see Sewing the Columns on pages 26–28). Remove postable notes.

Quilt

Quilt your project using purple (or contrasting) top thread and bobbin thread to match the backing (see Quilting the Project on page 29). Quilt as shown below.

Quilting Diagram

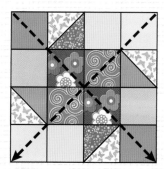

First pass

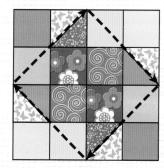

Second pass

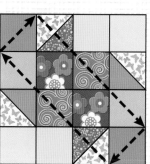

Third pass

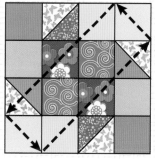

Fourth pass

ADD BORDERS

1 Add the inner and outer borders, courthouse-steps style, sides first, then top and bottom (see Adding Borders on pages 30 and 31). Add a line of outline stitching on the inside of the border, using the presser foot as a width guide, as described on page 31 if desired.

2 Trim the pillow top to 23" square.

FINISH

1 Fold the brown backing pieces in half, wrong sides together, and press. The folded pieces should measure 14" × 23".

2 Stack the folded backing pieces on top of the quilted pillow top, lining up the raw edges. Fold should be parallel. Pin in place.

3 Stitch all around the pillow using the needle-down function to pivot at the corners. Use ½" seam allowance, or to decrease the pointy effect at the corners of the pillow, grade the seam allowance, increasing the seam allowance gradually to ⅝" at corners and decreasing the seam allowance to ⅜" at the centers of the sides.

4 Turn the pillow cover right side out, poking the corners out with closed scissors. Insert a pillow to test the fit. Remove the pillow. If necessary, adjust any seams to add or reduce the ease. Trim the seams and clip the corners. Reinsert the pillow form, adding scrap batting to stuff corners as needed.

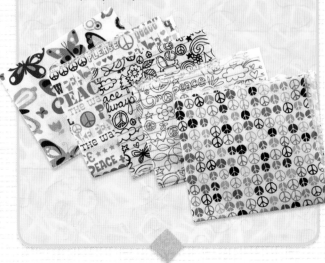

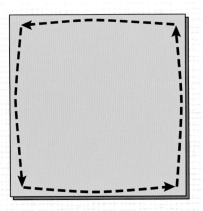

Stitching Diagram

Back of pillow

WHIMSICAL RAINBOW DOLL QUILT

This little quilt is the perfect size for your favorite young lady's 18" doll or for collectors' art dolls like the one shown, made by guest artist elinor peace bailey. Choose a spectrum of bright colors or historical hues (such as 1930s feed-sack prints or Victorian florals) to coordinate with your special doll.

Finished quilt: 16" × 21"
Sample stitched by Robin Fenn

24" doll made by elinor peace bailey using her Pretty Girl doll pattern, www.epbdolls.net

FABRIC AND NOTIONS:

- ⅛ yd. (or a scrap at least 4" square) of pink with red dots (half-square triangle units)
- ⅛ yd. (or a scrap at least 4" square) of lime green with turquoise crescent moons (half-square triangle units)
- ¼ yd. black with multicolor dots (squares and half-square triangle units)
- ⅛ yd. (or a scrap at least 6" square) yellow-orange print (squares)
- ⅛ yd. (or a scrap at least 6" square) red with pink swirls print (squares)
- ⅛ yd. (or a scrap at least 6" square) purple with pink dots (squares)
- ⅛ yd. (or a scrap at least 6" square) lime with turquoise dots (squares)
- ⅛ yd. turquoise tonal print (half-square triangle units)
- ⅛ yd. fuchsia print (squares)
- ¾ yd. flannel (backing/binding)
- Batting: 21" × 27", ultrathin
- Thread for piecing in neutral color
- Thread for bobbin to match backing
- Contrast thread for quilting
- ¼" wide Steam-A-Seam 2 fusible web tape

In This Project:
Thermore Ultra Thin batting by Hobbs

TOOLS AND SUPPLIES:

- Basic 90-Minute Quilt tools (see pages 8–13)
- 4"–6½" square ruler
- 3" square ruler
- 6" × 24" ruler

PREPARE

Prewash the flannel. Prewash the other fabrics if desired.

CUT

- One 4" square from the pink with red dots
- One 4" square from the lime green with turquoise crescent moons
- Two 4" squares, four 3" squares and one strip 3" × 34" from the black with multicolor dots
- Four 3" squares from the yellow-orange print
- Four 3" squares from the red with pink swirls print
- Four 3" squares from the purple with pink dots
- Four 3" squares from the lime with turquoise dots
- One strip 3" × 34" from the turquoise tonal print
- Eight 3" squares from the fuchsia print

MAKE HALF-SQUARE TRIANGLE UNITS

1 Make two half-square triangle units from the pink and black 4" squares using Method 1 (see page 17). Trim to 3" square.

2 Make two half-square triangle units from the lime green and black 4" squares using Method 1 (see page 17). Trim to 3" square.

3 Make sixteen half-square triangle units from the turquoise tonal print and the black strips using Method 2 (see page 18). Trim to 3" square.

LAYOUT

Lay out the squares, referring to the layout quilt image on page 101.

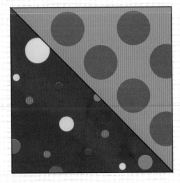

Make 2

Make 16

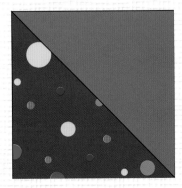

Make 2

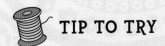

TIP TO TRY

For scale-size drape, use very thin batting or eliminate the batting and simply stitch the squares directly to the flannel backing. To self-bind this project without batting, follow the Self-Binding directions, omitting steps 3–6 (see pages 32–35).

Sew

1 Label and sew the squares into columns. This creates six columns with eight squares in each. Press seam allowances (up for even columns, down for odd columns).

2 Place the flannel backing on a flat surface, right side down, and center the batting on top. Mark the center of this batting/backing unit.

3 Line up the left-hand edge of Column 4 with the marked center of the batting/backing and pin in place.

4 Sew all the columns down (see Sewing the Columns on pages 26–28). Remove postable notes.

Quilt

Quilt your project (see Quilting the Project on page 29).

Bind

Trim the backing to 1¾" and the batting to a scant ½" and complete the self-binding (see Self-Binding on pages 32–35).

CONSIDER THIS!

Abby and Hayley wanted quilts for their historical dolls, so their quilter-mom taught them how to make some as their beginner quilting projects.

Abby said, "I chose these fabrics to go with my American Girl doll, Samantha, because the pink, maroon and blue flowered fabrics had a Victorian look."

Hayley selected the reproduction fabrics for her historical doll because "I found out that the Aunt Grace fabrics were copies of actual fabrics that might have been used when Emily was growing up during World War II."

They are both so excited about their new quilting skills that they are making more quilts like these to go with the rest of the historical dolls in their collections.

VARIATIONS: DREAMS OF DELFT PLACE MAT AND COASTER

To make this place mat variation, choose four values of crisp blue and white for a Dutch-themed place mat, or use colors in four different values to match your table decor. The four half-square triangle units in the center of the doll quilt layout have been switched with the corner squares of the placemat so they will not be hidden under the plate. As a final touch, the coordinating coaster has a fragrant surprise!

PLACE MAT

MATERIALS

- Fat or long eighth of white tonal; Cut four 3" squares and two 4" squares
- Fat or long quarter of light blue print; Cut six 3" squares and six 4" squares
- Fat or long quarter of medium blue print; Cut fourteen 3" squares and two 4" squares
- Fat or long quarter dark blue print; Cut four 3" squares and ten 4" squares
- 100% Cotton batting (a hot plate may melt a polyester batting)

SEW

1 Make four half-square triangle units from two 4" squares of white and two 4" squares of dark blue prints.

2 Make four half-square triangle units from two 4" squares of medium and two 4" squares of dark blue prints.

3 Make twelve half-square triangle units from six 4" squares of light and six 4" squares of dark blue prints.

4 Lay out according to the image above and construct as for the doll quilt.

COASTER

MATERIALS

- Four 2½" squares of assorted coordinating fabrics (Four-Patch)
- Two 4½" × 5½" pieces of coordinating fabrics (backing)
- Two pieces of cotton batting: one 5" × 5", one 3¼" × 3¼"
- A teaspoon or more of dried lavender, rose petals or other fragrant flower/herb

SEW

1 Stitch 2½" squares into a Four-Patch. Press. Place the Four-Patch on top of the 5" square of batting and quilt as desired. Trim the batting flush with the squares.

2 Fold the two backing pieces in half, wrong sides together, and press. The folded pieces should measure 4½" × 2¾".

3 Stack the backing pieces on top of the quilted coaster top, lining up raw edges, right sides together with folds parallel, and pin.

4 Stitch all around the coaster using the needle-down function to pivot at corners with a ¼" seam allowance.

5 Trim the corners. Turn the coaster right side out, poking corners out with closed scissors. Add dried flowers and insert 3¼" × 3¼" batting. Repeat to make additional coasters. Replenish the dried flowers as needed.

CELEBRATE!

This festive wall hanging makes a charming holiday decoration. Choose red and green for Christmas or add black for Kwanzaa. For Hanukkah, use royal-blue for the candle and golden ochres, tans and browns for the background—make nine for a menorah! To create a larger wall hanging for a place of worship or community space, simply cut larger squares.

Finished quilt: 16" × 42"
Sample stitched by Deborah Renfrow

FABRIC AND NOTIONS:

- 4–6 assorted yellow-gold tonal fabric squares or scraps
- 15–22 assorted maroon/red/rose tonal fabric squares or scraps ranging from very dark to very light values
- 30–45 assorted green tonal fabric squares or scraps ranging from very dark to very light values
- ¼ yd. medium red tonal print (inner border)
- ¼ yd. golden tan batik (outer border)
- ⅝ yd. striped fabric for bias binding
- ⅞ yd. standard width flannel (backing)
- Scrap of coordinating fabric large enough to cut a 4" × 13½" rectangle (rod pocket)
- Batting: about 19" × 45"
- Thread for piecing in neutral color
- Thread for bobbin to match backing
- Contrast thread for quilting

In This Project:
Selected fabrics from Keepsake Quilting's charm packs (Nancy Halvorsen, Thimbleberries, Christmas and Heirloom); Bali Batik border yardage from Keepsake Quilting; Jinny Beyer cottons and Mayfair flannel backing by RJR; Hobbs Heirloom Cotton Batting; Sulky Blendables thread color #4117

TOOLS AND SUPPLIES:

- Basic 90-Minute Quilt tools (see pages 8–13)
- 6" × 24" ruler
- 2½" square ruler with diagonal center markings

PREPARE

Prewash the flannel backing. Piece to make a 20" × 46" backing. (This seam can be positioned at the top and covered with the rod pocket/casing.) Prewash other fabrics if desired.

CUT

- Two 2½" squares from the yellow/gold fabrics
- Twenty-two maroon/red/rose 2½" squares in value range from dark to light (*I cut twelve additional maroon/red/rose squares for flexibility in designing*)
- Forty green 2½" squares in value range from dark to light (*I cut fourteen additional green squares for flexibility in designing*)
- Three 1½" wide strips from the medium red tonal fabric (inner border)
- Three 2½" wide strips from the golden-tan batik fabric (outer border)
- One 4" × 13½" rectangle from the coordinating fabric (rod pocket)

Note: The additional squares or triangles for the half square triangle units will be cut after the layout process in order to determine which fabrics are best in these positions.

LAYOUT

1 Arrange the squares on a flat design surface, referring to the layout quilt image on page 105 to create the look shown, leaving the five half-square triangle unit areas empty.

2 Determine which fabrics to use for the half-square triangle units. Stitch by either using 4" squares (see Method #1 on page 17) or use the method below if you prefer to use all different fabrics for the triangles in the half-square triangle units or if you have only small scraps left over. Trim the half-square triangle units to 2½" squares.

OPTIONAL: MAKE HALF-SQUARE TRIANGLE UNITS FROM TRIANGLES

1 Cut right triangles that measure 3½" × 3½" on each short side. Cut one rose, five dark green and four golden yellow triangles.

2 Following the layout, pair up triangles and stitch together along the long sides. Press open and trim to make finished 2½" half-square triangle units.

3 Place the half-square triangle units in the appropriate positions.

SEW

1 Label and sew the squares into columns. This creates four columns with seventeen squares in each. Press seam allowances (up for even columns, down for odd columns).

2 Place the flannel backing on a flat surface, right side down. If you hav epieced the backing, position the seam at the top so you can cover it with the rod pocket/casing. Center the batting on top. Mark the center of this batting/backing unit.

3 Line up the left side of Column 3 with the marked center of the batting/backing unit, and pin in place.

4 Sew all the columns down (see Sewing the Columns on pages 26–28). Remove postable notes.

QUILT

1 Pin all the raw edges of the squares through the batting/backing unit to stabilize them.

2 Use contrasting top thread and bobbin thread to match the backing. Referring to the quilting diagram on page 105, start in corner, backstitch and stitch straight across each square, corner to corner, on the diagonal. Leaving the needle in the down position makes it easier to pivot at the corners. Stitch only to within ¼" of raw edges on outside squares as shown.

3 Backstitch when you get to a corner of the quilt. Begin the second pass in either remaining corner and stitch as in Step 2 so that each square is quilted with an X. Remove pins.

BORDERS

1 Add the inner red border, courthouse-steps style, sides first (see Adding Borders on pages 30 and 31). Add the golden tan outer border in the same manner. Outline-quilt a line around the inner edge of the gold border if desired.

2 Staystitch the edges with a narrow zigzag within a ¼" seam allowance. Trim to 16" × 42".

ROD POCKET (CASING)

1 Fold the rod pocket fabric under ½" on the two short sides and either long side, wrong sides together. Topstitch around the three sides. Pin the wrong side of the rod pocket to the center top of the quilt back, lining up raw edges.

2 Add bias binding (see Making/Attaching Bias Binding on pages 36–39). (Rod pocket/casing will be caught in the seam for bias binding.)

3 Handstitch the bottom edge of the rod pocket.

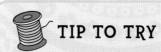

TIP TO TRY

Make longer or shorter candles by adding or removing rows of squares.

Quilting Diagram

End   Start

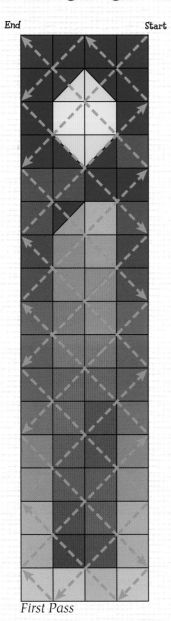

First Pass

LAYOUT QUILT

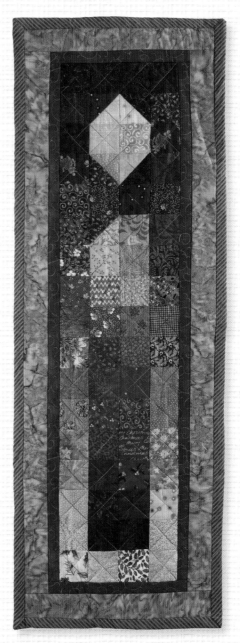

A PASSION FOR PLUM

Stunning glass buttons and three-dimensional half-square triangle units add sparkle and interest to this sophisticated-looking art quilt. The motion of the pinwheel design seems to dance through the luscious purples and warm ochres of the suede-look cottons. The effective use of hand-dyed gradation fabrics makes a simple design look much more complex and adds lots of textural interest.

Finished quilt: 32" × 32"
Sample stitched by Deborah Renfrow

FABRIC AND NOTIONS:

- Set of eight gradation fat quarters (choose a gradation that goes from very dark to very light)
- ½ yd. coordinating fabric (border)
- 1½ yds. coordinating flannel (backing/binding)
- Thread for piecing in neutral color
- Thread for bobbin to match backing
- Transparent monofilament thread* (smoke color) for quilting
- One large and four small glass buttons for embellishment
- Metallic thread (optional)
- ¼" wide Steam-A-Seam 2 fusible web tape

*I use MonoPoly monofilament thread because it doesn't tangle.

In This Project:

Cherrywood Grand Canyon Eight Step gradations; Chocolate Ginkgo Tonal by Kona Bay; Stonehenge flannel by Northcott; Nature-Fil bamboo batting by Fairfield; Sulky Blendables thread; MonoPoly invisible polyester thread (smoke) by Superior threads; Glass buttons by www.ascuteasabutton.com; Sliver gold metallic thread by Sulky

TOOLS AND SUPPLIES:

- Basic 90-Minute Quilt tools (see pages 8–13)
- 6" × 24" ruler
- 4½" square ruler

PREPARE

Prewash backing/binding flannel. Trim to 41" × 41". Prewash hand-dyed fabrics if desired. Use Synthrapol when washing hand-dyed fabrics.

Make a fabric chart with values 1 (darkest) to 8 (lightest) of fabric for reference. Tape a small swatch from the selvedge to the chart below for reference. (Value #5 is not used in this project.)

CUT

- Two 5½" squares from Value #1/darkest (label the stack with a postable note: Value #1)
- Eight 4½" squares from Value #2 (label the stack: Value #2)
- Eight 4½" squares from Value #3 (label the stack: Value #3)
- Twelve 4½" squares from Value #4 (label the stack: Value #4)
- Eight 4½" squares from Value #6 (label the stack: Value #6)
- Eight 4½" squares from Value #7 (label the stack: Value #7)
- Two 5½" squares from Value #8/lightest (label the stack: Value #8)
- Four strips 3¼" wide from the border print fabric

Value 1 (darkest)	tape swatch here	Value 2	tape swatch here	Value 3	tape swatch here	Value 4	tape swatch here	Value 5	tape swatch here	Value 6	tape swatch here	Value 7	tape swatch here	Value 8 (lightest)	tape swatch here

Make Half-Square Triangle Units

1 Pair up each of the light (Value #8) 5½" squares with the dark (Value #1) 5½" squares. Make four half-square triangle units. Set aside.

2 Press the following in half, diagonally, pressing carefully to avoid stretching, and spraying with water to form a flat, crisp fold:
- Four 4½" squares—Value #2
- Eight 4½" squares—Value #3

3 Pair four Value #2 pressed triangles with four Value #4 squares, and pin them together (corner blocks).

4 Pair four Value #3 pressed triangles with four Value #4 squares, and pin them together, lining up raw edges (blocks adjacent to corner blocks).

5 Pair four Value #3 pressed triangles with four Value #6 squares, and pin them together (blocks for ends of pinwheel).

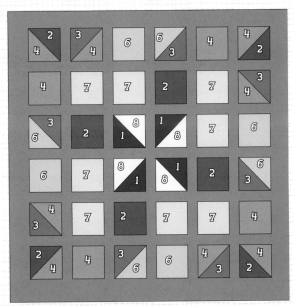

Use this grayscale diagram to help arrange your gradated fabrics.

Layout

Arrange the squares on a flat design surface, referring to the grayscale diagram (below) or the layout quilt image on page 109 to create the look shown.

Sew

1 Label and sew the squares into columns. This creates six columns with six squares in each. Press seam allowances (up for even columns, down for odd columns).

2 Place the flannel backing on a flat surface, right side down, and center the batting on top. Mark the center of this batting/backing unit.

3 Line up the left side of Column 4 with the marked center of the batting/backing unit, and pin in place.

4 Sew all the columns down (see Sewing the Columns on pages 26–28). Remove postable notes.

Quilt

Use transparent smoke monofilament top thread and bobbin thread to match the backing. Stitch in the ditch across all horizontal seams, backstitching at the beginning and end of each pass.

Borders

Add the borders courthouse-steps style—sides first, then top and bottom (see Adding Borders on pages 30 and 31). Add optional quilting to the inner edge of the border with metallic thread if desired.

Bind and Finish

1 Trim the backing to 3½" and the batting to 1¼" and complete the self-binding (see Self-Binding on pages 32–35).

2 Embellish with buttons as shown.

Layout Quilt

ENCHANTED POSIES

Cuddle your favorite toddler in the fanciful flowers of this charming quilt. Or hang it on an infant's wall for a delightful decoration until they grow too big for enchanted dreams about cheerful garden critters.

Finished quilt: 36½" × 54½"
Sample stitched by the author

FABRIC AND NOTIONS:

- Panel fabric with seven or more 9½" square panels
- ½ yd. yellow floral fabric (squares for Four-Patch)
- ⅓ yd. lilac floral fabric (squares for Four-Patch)
- ¾ yd. pink floral fabric (squares for Four-Patch and outer border)
- ¼ yd. purple floral fabric (inner border)
- 1⅞ yd. light gold watercolor flannel (backing/binding)
- Batting: Crib size (or about 40" × 65")
- Thread for piecing in neutral color
- Thread for bobbin to match backing
- Contrast thread for quilting
- ½" wide Steam-A-Seam 2 fusible web tape

In This Project:
The Secret Life of Fairies collection by Salina Yoon for RJR Fabrics; flannel backing/binding: RJR's Handspray flannel in pale gold; Fairfield's Nature-Fil bamboo batting; Sulky 4102 Spring Garden Blendables thread

TOOLS AND SUPPLIES:

- Basic 90-Minute Quilt tools (see pages 8–13)
- 6" × 24" ruler
- 9½" square ruler with diagonal center markings (for accurate fussy-cutting)

PREPARE

Prewash the flannel (should be at least 42" wide after preshrinking). Prewash the other fabrics as desired.

CUT

- Fussy-cut motifs using a 9½" square ruler. A revolving mat is helpful. (This collection offers eight possible motifs, and the quilt uses seven. I cut out all eight and played with the arrangement to determine which seven I wanted to use.)
- Two 5½" wide strips plus two 5½" squares from the yellow floral fabric
- One 5½" wide strip plus one 5½" square from the lilac floral fabric
- One 5½" wide strip and one 5½" square from the pink floral fabric
- Four 3¼" wide strips from the pink floral fabric
- Four 1¼" wide strips from the purple floral fabric

VARIATION

If you have selected a panel print with smaller images than in the shown quilt, just add a log cabin border to make the panels 9½" square. If your panels are larger, they can still be used by selecting a 9½" square portion of the design to use for the panel block.

Make Four-Patch Units

1 Stitch together one 5½" wide yellow floral strip with the 5½" pink floral strip along the long edge.

2 Stitch together one 5½" wide yellow floral strip with the 5½" lilac floral strip along the long edge. Press the seam allowances toward the yellow floral fabric.

3 Subcut seven 5½" crosswise units from each stripped pair.

Combining three different colorways of the same print offers more interest, texture and depth of color than a single fabric—just like a real garden!

4 Stitch one yellow and pink unit to one yellow and lilac unit, positioning the yellow squares diagonally across from each other, to make a Four-Patch.

5 Trim to a perfect 9½" square with the ruler.

> ◆ Note: You can make seven Four-Patches from the strips. Use the extra 5½" squares to make the eighth Four-Patch.

Layout

Position the Four-Patch units and the cut motif squares on a flat surface, arranging as shown or as desired.

Sew

1 Label and sew the squares into columns. This creates three columns with five blocks in each. Press seam allowances (up for even columns, down for odd columns).

2 Place the flannel backing on a flat surface, right side down, and center the batting on top. Mark the center of this batting/backing unit.

3 Line up the center of Column 2 with the marked center of the batting/backing unit and pin in place.

4 Sew down Columns 1 and 3 (see Sewing the Columns on pages 26–28). Remove postable notes.

Quilt

Quilt your project using contrasting top thread and bobbin thread to match the backing (see Quilting the Project on page 29). Quilt "X's" as instructed on page 29, adding four horizontal lines of stitch-in-the-ditch quilting, or quilt as desired.

Borders

1 Add 1¼" wide purple strips, courthouse-steps style, to the top and bottom of the quilt, reserving scraps. Use these scraps to lengthen the remaining 1¼" wide purple strips. Then add these strips to the sides of the quilt.

2 Repeat with the 3¼" wide pink floral strips for the wider border. Add an outline of quilting stitches close to the seam if desired.

Bind

Trim the backing to 3" and the batting to 1" and complete the self-binding (see Self-Binding on pages 32–35).

BROCADED CARP

The translation of the Japanese word for the ornamental koi is "brocaded carp." This shimmering fish is popular in Asia as a symbol of love and friendship, and in feng shui practice it represents wealth and success. This art quilt is a stunning home decoration or gift item and offers an opportunity to experiment with your choice of machine quilting techniques.

Finished quilt: 33" × 42"
Sample stitched by the author

114

FABRIC AND NOTIONS:

- ⅝ yd. koi fish panel type print (area selected for use is 17" × 26" finished, trim size is 19" × 28")
- ¼ yd. black tonal (inner border)
- ¼ yd. charcoal tonal (outer strips in striped border)
- ¼ yd. rust tonal (inner strips in striped border)
- ¼ yd. teal with metallic gold tonal (center strips in striped border)
- ¾ yd. or more large Asian floral print (outer border background—exact amount depends on the length of the repeat and the look desired)
- ¾ yd. muslin
- Batting: two pieces, 21" × 30" and 40" × 52", ultrathin
- 1⅝ yds. of black tonal flannel (backing/binding)
- Thread for piecing in neutral color
- Thread for bobbin to match backing flannel
- Thread for quilting (use metallic thread and a machine needle for metallic thread if desired)
- Size 8 glass beads, pearlized peach
- Swarovski hot fix crystal rhinestones from size 6ss through size 20ss in coordinating colors
- ¼" wide Steam-A-Seam 2 fusible web tape

In This Project:
Fabrics by Kona Bay; Fossil Fern flannel by Benartex; hot fix crystals and setter by Creative Crystals

TOOLS AND SUPPLIES:

- Basic 90-Minute Quilt tools (see pages 8–13)
- Cutting mats 18" × 24", 24" × 36"
- 6" × 24" ruler
- Chalk markers (two colors)
- 6" sewing gauge with movable slider
- Hot fix crystal rhinestone setter tool

PREPARE

Select the area of the panel print you wish to use. Measure and mark the finished size of your selected area with chalk. In this project, the finished size of the selected area was 17" × 26".

Add 1" all around the perimeter (which adds 2" to each dimension) and draw this trim line in a different color chalk. Use a trifold ruler (see Tip To Try on page 21) to make sure the corners are square. This panel was trimmed to 19" × 28". If you choose a different panel, measure the size and add 2" all around to the size of your selected finished area. You will have to adjust the size of the backing, batting, background and borders to correspond with the size of your project.

Prewash and dry flannel and muslin. Flannel should be at least 40"/41" wide after prewashing and drying. Trim flannel to 54". Trim muslin to 21" × 30". Prewash the other fabrics as desired.

CUT

- Trim panel to 19" × 28"
- Three strips 1¾" wide from the darker black tonal fabric (inner border)
- Two strips 1¼" wide from the charcoal tonal fabric (outer border pieced stripe)
- Two strips 2" wide from the rust tonal fabric (outer border pieced stripe)
- One strip 5" wide from the teal and gold metallic tonal fabric (outer border pieced stripe)
- Two strips 12" wide from the large Asian floral fabric. Fussy-cut to include or avoid select areas of the pattern, if desired (border background)

Quilt the Panel

1 Place the muslin on a flat surface. Place the 26" × 36" piece of batting on top. Center the panel on top of the muslin and batting, and pin.

2 Using metallic thread, quilt as desired using regular stitching or free-motion quilting on your sewing machine. Use a longer stitch length and a metallic needle with metallic thread. Quilt areas as evenly as possible. Tie threads as needed. Leave some areas unquilted; plan to quilt them in Construct Step 3.

3 Trim the panel to 18" x 27" (one inch larger than the original determined size).

Make Stripped Outer Border Units

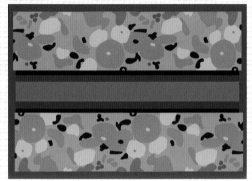

1 Stitch the strips together in the order shown above, pressing as you go to form a stripped panel.

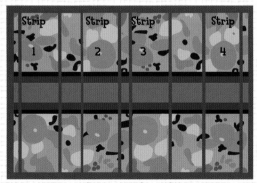

2 Fussy cross-cut four strips from the strip panel, each 6" wide, lining up the ruler so it is perpendicular to the stitched seams of the strata unit.

Construct

1 Place the flannel backing on a flat surface, right side down. Center the 36" × 48" piece of thin batting on top.

2 Center the quilted panel on the batting/backing unit and pin the panel in place.

3 Using bobbin thread to match the backing flannel, quilt the areas reserved earlier (Quilt Step 2) with coordinating thread to secure the quilted panel to backing.

4 Using a ½" seam allowance, stitch two of the 1¾" black inner border strips to the sides of the panel. Backstitch or tie off at the beginning and end of each seam. Trim excess length from strips after stitching. Add the black tonal border strips to the top and bottom in the same way, and trim.

5 Measure and mark the centers of the four sides of the panel unit with chalk.

6 Line up the centers of two of the stripped outer-border units with the marked centers on both sides of the center panel. Attach the borders to the quilt, courthouse-steps style, as in Step 4. Repeat with top and bottom.

Finish

1 Add additional quilting as desired.

2 Trim the backing to 3½" and the batting to 1¼" and add self-binding (see Self-Binding on pages 32–35).

3 Embellish the quilt by handstitching eighteen to twenty-four glass beads to the center panel of the quilt, especially in areas with minimal quilting. (This is for decoration as well as to secure the layers together.)

4 Following the manufacturer's directions, add hot fix crystals in assorted sizes of 6ss–20ss using a hot fix crystal setter.

SAIL AWAY, MONET

French impressionist Claude Monet painted many sailboats at Argenteuil in his numerous explorations of color and value relationships. Have fun stitching this nautical wall hanging or baby quilt while you explore value relationships and some basic fine art principles. The easy construction methods let you concentrate on training your eye to see more nuances in value relationships, which results in more success with values in future projects.

Finished quilt: 37½" × 47"
Sample stitched by Sarah Norman and Kathy Thompson

FABRIC AND NOTIONS:

- Assortment of batiks in blues, greens and purples in a range of light to dark values, 6½" squares or larger (sky, hull, water, reflections)
- ¼ yd. very pale yellow batik (for at least five 6½" squares) (sails)
- ¼ yd. medium/dark blue batik (inner border)
- ½ yd. light gold/blue batik (outer border)
- ⅝ yd. medium blue/green/purple (bias binding)
- Batting: Crib size (or about 40" × 51")
- 1¾ yd. standard width flannel (backing)
- Thread for piecing in neutral color
- Thread for bobbin to match backing flannel
- Thread for quilting

In This Project:

Batiks by Island Batik; Ro Gregg's Rock 'n Roll flannel by Northcott; Aurifil thread; Hobbs Heirloom cotton batting

TOOLS AND SUPPLIES:

- Basic 90-Minute Quilt tools (see pages 8–13)
- 5½" square ruler with diagonal marking
- 6½" square ruler

PREPARE

Wash and dry flannel. After washing, the standard width flannel should be at least 41" wide. Trim to 53" long.

Sort through fabrics to create value groups. You may want to stack and label the groups after you've sorted them:

- The very lightest light (pale yellow batik) is the fabric for the sails. Set it aside.
- Select the lightest blues for the sky and the darkest darks for the hull first because this establishes your limits on each end of the value scale. Choose three to five darks for the hull (darkest darks) and a range of light to medium values for the sky, from light blue at the horizon and gradating toward darker values farther up in the sky.

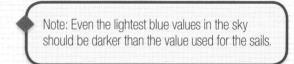

Note: Even the lightest blue values in the sky should be darker than the value used for the sails.

- Select fabrics for the reflection of the hull: This is the second darkest group—lighter than the hull, but darker than the water and sky.
- Select fabrics for the water: The value of the water is darker than the reflection of the sails and lighter than the reflection of the hull.

Make your best guess when first selecting these values. It's not possible to know if they are correct until squares are cut and placed in the layout. You can reevaluate and reposition the squares before committing to the design.

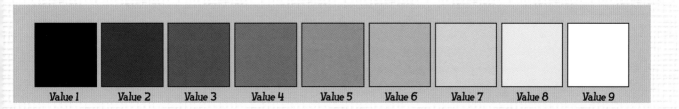

Value 1   Value 2   Value 3   Value 4   Value 5   Value 6   Value 7   Value 8   Value 9

Cut Squares
(Sky, Hull and Hull Reflections)

- Twenty-one (or more) 5½" squares from sky fabrics (Rows 1–6)

- Three 5½" squares from hull (Row 6)

- Three 5½" squares from hull-reflection fabrics that coordinate with hull fabric (Row 7)

- Three 5½" squares from assorted water fabrics (Rows 7 and 8)

> Note: Additional squares may be cut for more options in the design/layout process.

Cut Squares for Half-Square Triangle Units

- Five 6½" squares from sail fabric (Rows 2-5)

- Five (or more, if more colors are desired) 6½" squares from assorted middle-value sky fabrics (triangle sky shapes, Rows 2–5)

- One 6½" square from hull fabric (Row 6)

- One 6½" square from lightest sky fabric (Row 6)

- One 6½" square from lighter water fabric (Row 7)

- One 6½" square from hull-reflection fabric (Row 7)

- At least two (three were used in this sample) 6½" squares from water fabrics (Row 8)

- Two 6½" squares from sail-reflection fabrics (Row 8)

- Four strips 1⅛" wide (inner border)

- Four strips 3¼" wide (outer border)

- Cut and seam at least 5 yds. of 2⅝" wide bias binding

> Note: For this project, 6½" squares in sail or hull fabrics may be sliced diagonally to create triangles in instances where only one half-square triangle is needed in a particular color.

CONSIDER THIS!

A little knowledge of fine-art principles can richly enhance your pictorial quilts. In this nautical scene, I employed two landscape rules.

Values of the sky: In most daytime weather situations, the sky is lighter in value toward the horizon than it is overhead. In this quilt, the sky values are positioned accordingly.

Values in reflections: Many people believe that because water has a shiny surface, reflections have more value contrast that the actual object reflected. This is an illusion. A reflection actually has less contrast in value than the object it reflects. It is the sharpness of the edges in the reflection that creates the feel of a shiny look, not the value contrast.

When we look directly at an object, such as a sail, we see the full intensity of the color and value. In a reflection, the light from the sail must travel to the water and then to our eyes. The color and value of the sail loses intensity because its image takes a longer trip before it hits the optic nerve. So, lighter objects lose some of their intensity, or lightness, when we see them reflected in water and therefore appear slightly darker in the reflection.

Dark objects also lose their intensity when they are reflected. Therefore, the reflection of a dark object appears slightly lighter than the original object.

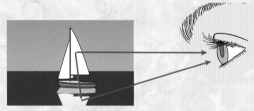

Find a place where you can look at objects reflected in still water on a sunny day, where lights and shadows are clearly visible, and you can confirm this fine art principal. The camera does not capture values in the same way that the eye sees them, so it's best to check this out in reality.

MAKE HALF-SQUARE TRIANGLE UNITS

1 Pair up the 6½" squares, using the layout quilt image on page 123 as a guide.

2 With a chalk marker, draw a diagonal line from corner to corner on the wrong side of one of the squares in each pair. (If only one half-square triangle unit in a particular pair of colors is needed, cut both squares along this diagonal and then stitch them together. Press and trim the square after stitching.)

3 Following the instructions on page 17, make the half-square triangle units. Trim each to a perfect 5½" square.

LAYOUT

Arrange the squares on a flat design surface, referring to the layout quilt image on page 123 to create the look shown. Label the top squares X and 1–5. The fabrics used in Column X need to work well with the adjacent fabrics in both Columns 1 and 5.

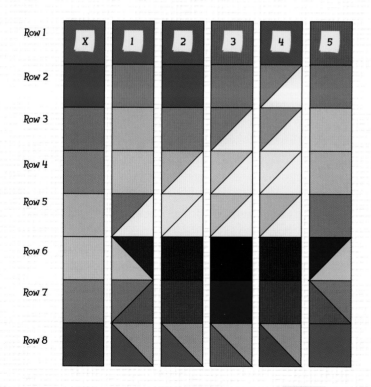

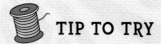
By squinting your eyes, your eyelashes act as a filter to simplify the perception of the overall tone of each value. This makes it easier to compare value relationships. I encourage my students to pretend their brain is a camera and take an imaginary black-and-white photo of the subject, in a range of gray values. Taking an actual photo of your subject matter or quilt on your design board and converting it to black-and-white in a graphic design program is another useful way to see values more clearly. Since the camera does not capture values in exactly the same way that the eye sees them, this technique is not completely accurate, but it can offer an overall impression of values.

Many quilters look at their fabric through colored glass to see correct values. However, this does not give accurate results for fabrics that are the same color as the glass used.

The best way to learn values is to give your eyes the opportunity to practice. Next time you are at a boring red light or waiting in line at the grocery store, compare value relationships around you, noticing which colors appear to be lighter and darker values, and imagining where they might fall on a value scale.

Soon your eye will be trained to automatically notice an object's value as well as its color.

Sew

1 Stitch the squares together in order in each column, being careful to preserve the orientation of half-square triangle units. This creates six columns with eight squares in each. After stitching, lay the columns out in their appropriate positions, placing Column X on the left, and check that the original placement of the squares has been preserved. To doublecheck how the colors will coordinate after trimming, place Column X next to Column 5.

2 Press seam allowances up (toward the top square with the label) on even-numbered columns and the X column. Press seam allowances down on odd-numbered columns.

3 Slice the X unit vertically. Label one strip X1 and the other X2.

4 Place the flannel backing on a flat surface, right side down. Place the batting on top, centered approximately on the backing. Mark the center of this batting/backing unit.

5 Line up the center of Column 3 with the approximate center of the batting/backing unit and pin it in place.

6 Sew all the columns down, including X1 and X2 (see Sewing the Columns on pages 26–28). Stitch X1 to the left of Column 1 and X2 to the right of Column 5. Remove postable notes.

Quilt

1 Pin the raw edges of the squares through the batting/backing unit to stabilize them. Increase stitch length if desired. Use contrasting top thread and bobbin thread to match the backing. Quilt as desired or as follows.

2 Stitch in the ditch where the sky meets the ocean, between Rows 6 and 7.

3 Draw five horizontal quilting lines with chalk or wash-away fabric marker, spacing them apart as shown on the diagram on page 123. Graduating the amount of space between the lines gives the illusion of perspective. Stitch.

4 Draw diagonal stitching lines as shown. Stitch.

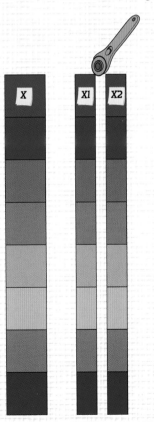

Note: Most of these lines run diagonally from one corner of a square to another. In areas where it is not possible to measure it this way, simply draw parallel lines with the ruler. These parallel diagonal lines are about 3½" apart.

Borders

1 Add the inner, dark blue border, courthouse-steps style (see Adding Borders on pages 30 and 31).

2 Add the outer border, courthouse-steps style, sides first and then the top and bottom. Outline quilt the border if desired. Trim.

Bind

Finish with bias binding (see Making/Attaching Bias Binding on pages 36–39). Add a rod pocket to hang if desired (see page 104).

Quilting Diagram and Layout Quilt

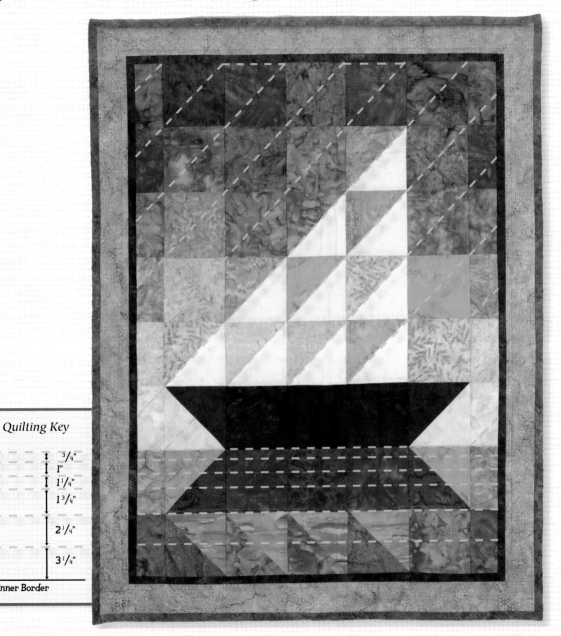

Quilting Key

	$3/4"$
	$1"$
	$1^1/_4"$
	$1^3/_4"$
	$2^1/_4"$
	$3^1/_4"$
Inner Border	

FOREVER IN BLUE JEANS - RECYCLED!

This "green" wall organizer is fun to make from discarded blue jeans. Even the batting has been recycled from plastic bottles! Use this great pocket organizer to hold cosmetics, sewing or craft supplies, or kids' games and toys.

Finished quilt: 32" × 32"
Sample stitched by the author

FABRIC AND NOTIONS:

- Four to six medium to lightweight denim garments with decorative detailing in values of light, medium and dark denim (Note the value range of denims on page 124.)
- ¼ yd. lightweight red denim 59/60" wide (or try cutting long pieces from pant legs; wrong side of fabric is used in sample) (borders)
- 36½" × 36½" square thin, recycled batting (appropriate to quilt up to 12" apart)
- 1¼ yd. coordinating or contrasting flannel (backing/binding)
- Scraps from garments or ¼ yd. of light-to-medium-weight denim yardage (for piecing, as needed)
- Thread for piecing in neutral color
- Thread for bobbin to match backing flannel
- *Optional*: Contrast thread for outline quilting
- ¼" wide Steam-A-Seam 2 fusible web tape
- *Optional*: hot-fix crystals and applicator, buttons

In This Project:
Dream Green batting by Quilters Dream (made from recycled plastic bottles); Swarovski hot-fix crystals and applicator by Creative Crystal

TOOLS AND SUPPLIES:

- Basic 90-Minute Quilt tools (see pages 8–13)
- 8½" × 24" ruler
- 8½" square ruler
- Very sharp scissors
- Very sharp rotary cutter
- Long, sharp, sturdy pins
- Machine needle for denim
- Walking foot or even feed function
- *Optional*: Jean-a-ma-jig tool

PREPARE

Prewash and dry jeans, denim fabric and flannel. Trim flannel to 40" × 40" square. Insert a denim needle into the machine.

DESIGN THREE COLUMNS

> Note: Use the diagram on page 127 and the photos on pages 124 and 126 as design guides. Read all of the instructions before cutting.

1 Select the motif areas desired (patch pockets, flap pockets, side pockets, key pockets, seams, loops, designer tags, buttons, yokes, embroidered areas and other garment detailing may be included). Motif areas may be measured with chalk or rough cut first to approximately 9½" wide, and then trimmed to 8½" wide. If the desired area of the garment is too small, add pieces to extend.

2 Lay out cut motifs on a flat design board, arranging as desired. The center is a good place for a focal point such as embroidery. Plan to stagger any horizontal seams at least ½" apart for easier construction. Be sure pocket top openings are at least ½" from any raw edges so they don't get caught in the seam allowances. When rough cutting a design interest area, a pocket may be cut across the bottom. Stitching it to the adjacent piece will close the pocket again. Plan to add embellishments such as decorative buttons or hot-fix crystals to areas that seem empty of design elements or that have holes or imperfections that need to be covered.

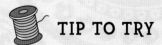

TIP TO TRY

Children's and toddlers' jeans or denim dresses have lots of decorative embroidery motifs and embellishments. Look for pockets and design elements that will fit in an 8" wide area. Garage sales and thrift shops are great sources—I got the garments used here for 99 cents each!

Sew

1 Extend widths of narrower pieces to 8½" wide by adding pieces of lightweight denim or scraps from cut-up garments. This piecing may be standard piecing, or you may simply place raw edges on top of other pieces and stitch a lapped seam, allowing the raw edges of one fabric to lap over the other.

2 Construct three pieced columns, 8½" wide × 24½" long, by piecing together selected motif areas. Press seams in any direction they naturally seem to fall. Topstitch seams as desired.

> Note: It is not necessary to carefully cover all the seams —after all, many jeans have rips on purpose!

3 Carefully trim away any layers of fabric not needed, such as excess lining in pocket areas. Trim away overcast seams leaving only the construction seam intact since these jeans will not be receiving stress.

4 Place the flannel backing on a flat surface, right-side down. Place the batting on top, centering it approximately.

5 Line up the center of Column 2 with the marked center of the batting/backing unit and pin it in place.

6 Sew down Columns 1 and 3 (see Sewing the Columns on pages 26–28).

Borders

1 Cut two border strips 3" wide × 26" long and two border strips 3" wide × 30" long.

2 Pin the two shorter border strips to the sides, lining up the long, raw edges. Stitch with ¼" seam allowance, through batting and backing, backstitching at the beginning and end of the seam. Flip the border strips open. Press carefully, avoiding contact with the batting.

3 Add remaining border strips to the top and bottom in the same manner.

4 Add outline quilting on the inner edge of the denim border, close to the seam: Move the needle position to the left, slightly lengthen the stitch length and use the edge of the presser foot for a guide.

5 Generously pin the outside raw edges of the denim border and staystitch through the batting and backing, within ⅛" of the raw edge, to stabilize.

Bind

Trim the backing to 3½" and the batting to 1¼" and complete the self-binding (see Self-Binding on pages 32–35).

Embellishments

Add buttons, hot-fix crystals or other embellishments as desired. When sewing on buttons, be sure to stitch through only the top layer on pockets so they aren't stitched closed!

VARIATION: DENIM ORGANIZER MADE WITH 6" SQUARES

LAYOUT DIAGRAM

Note: The red dotted lines show the position of the three staggered horizontal seams.

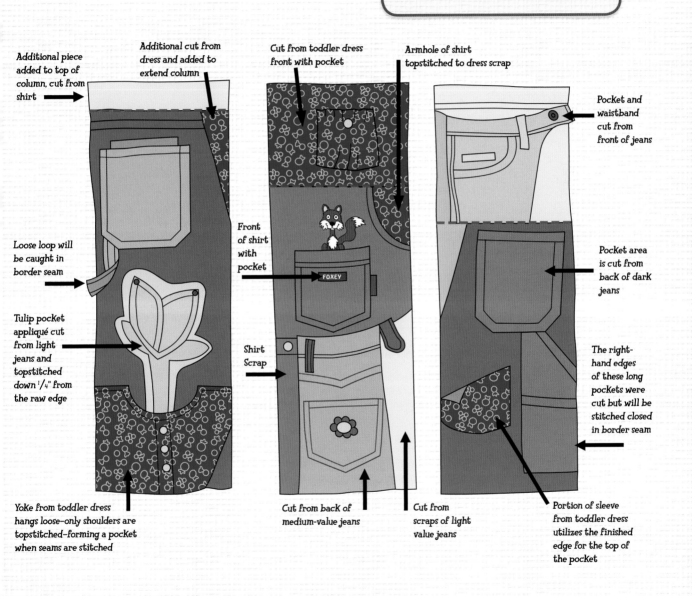

Additional piece added to top of column, cut from shirt

Additional cut from dress and added to extend column

Cut from toddler dress front with pocket

Armhole of shirt topstitched to dress scrap

Pocket and waistband cut from front of jeans

Loose loop will be caught in border seam

Tulip pocket appliqué cut from light jeans and topstitched down ¼" from the raw edge

Front of shirt with pocket

Shirt Scrap

Pocket area is cut from back of dark jeans

The right-hand edges of these long pockets were cut but will be stitched closed in border seam

Yoke from toddler dress hangs loose—only shoulders are topstitched—forming a pocket when seams are stitched

Cut from back of medium-value jeans

Cut from scraps of light value jeans

Portion of sleeve from toddler dress utilizes the finished edge for the top of the pocket

FOXEY

FLORALIA TABLECLOTH

The ancient Roman holiday of Floralia was a lavish spring festival in honor of Flora, the goddess of flowers. Dancing celebrants wore colorful garments and floral wreaths to pay homage to their goddess. An assortment of big and bold fabric designs and clever placement of half-square triangle units give this simple springtime quilt an exciting and complex look!

Finished quilt: 50" × 50"
Sample stitched by Robin Fenn

FABRIC AND NOTIONS:

- 1½ yds. large teal/periwinkle/pink floral print (fussy-cut squares)
- 1½ yds. large lime/blue/yellow floral print (fussy-cut squares and border rectangles)
- ⅓ yd. pale yellow tonal (stripped half-square triangle units, inner border)
- 1 yd. blue/teal medium floral print (half-square triangles and outer border)
- Fat quarter lime/white small floral print (stripped half-square triangles and Four-Patch)
- Fat quarter lilac/rose mini floral/berries print (Four-Patch)
- Fat quarter pink/lilac medium floral print (half-square triangles)
- Fat quarter lilac/white small floral print (half-square triangles)
- Fat quarter teal/periwinkle mini floral/berries print (half-square triangles)
- Fat quarter light teal/lilac vine print (half-square triangles)
- Fat quarter yellow/white small floral print (half-square triangles)
- Fat quarter yellow/lime vine print (stripped half-square triangles)
- 3½ yds. yellow tonal flannel (backing/binding)
- Batting: about 55" square, ultrathin
- Thread for piecing in neutral color
- Thread for bobbin to match backing
- Contrast thread for quilting
- ¼" wide Steam-A-Seam 2 double stick fusible web tape

Note: ⅓ yd. of fabric may be substituted for a fat quarter. Follow all cutting instructions, except when two 22" strips are cut from a fat quarter. Instead, simply cut one width-of-fabric strip from your yardage.

WOF=width-of-fabric; the width of fabric is the distance from one selvedge edge to the other.

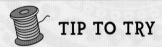

TIP TO TRY

If desired, purchase additional yardage to make coordinating napkins. ½ yd. will make two single-layer napkins or one reversible napkins. Finish the edges by serging, with a rolled hem or with bias binding.

In This Project:
Fat quarter sets and additional yardages from two colorways of the Elizabeth Anne collection by Alex Anderson, yellow and white tonal from Mother Goose & Friends, and yellow flannel all from P&B Textiles; Thermore batting by Hobbs; Sulky 12 wt. Blendables thread #4120 Springtime

TOOLS AND SUPPLIES:

- Basic 90-Minute Quilt tools (see pages 8–13)
- 6½" × 24" ruler
- 6½" square ruler with center markings (for accurate fussy-cutting)

PREPARE

Prewash the flannel. Prewash other fabrics as desired.

Cut flannel in half, seam it and trim to create a 56"/57" square. (This will be trimmed later.)

CUT

> Note: If you are using ⅓ yards instead of fat quarters, cut one strip from selvedge to selvedge (instead of cutting two 22" long strips).

• Fussy-cut nine 6½" squares from the large teal/periwinkle/pink floral print, centering the desired motifs within the 6½" square.

• Fussy-cut eight 6½" squares from the lime/blue/yellow floral print, centering motifs within the 6½" square. Cut four 18½" × 3½" center border strips from the fabric that remains after fussy-cutting is completed.

• Two 3½" × 22" and two 4" × 22" strips from the lime/white small floral (Four-Patch, stripped half-square triangles)

• Two 3½" × 22" strips from the lilac/rose mini floral/berries print (Four-Patch)

• One 1¾" × WOF strip (diagonally pieced half-square triangle units) and five 1⅜" × WOF strips (inner border) from the pale yellow tonal

• Two 5½" wide × 22" strips from the pink/lilac medium floral print (stripped half-square triangle units)

• Three 5½" × 22" lilac/white small floral print (half-square triangles)

• Three 5½" × 22" teal/periwinkle mini floral/berries print (half-square triangles)

• Three 5½" × 22" light teal/lilac vine print (half-square triangles)

• Three 5½" × 22" yellow/white small floral print (half-square triangles)

• Three 5½" × 22" strips from the yellow/lime vine print (stripped half-square triangles)

• Two 5½" × WOF strips from the blue/teal medium floral print. Subcut in half to pair with yellow-with-lime vine print strips (half-square triangles).

• Four 3½" × WOF strips from the blue/teal medium floral print. Subcut from each strip one 14" long strip and one 19" long strip.

TIP TO TRY

When using motif fabrics, if you are not sure if you have enough yardage to fussy-cut all the motifs you want, mark all the selected squares with a chalk marker before cutting.

MAKE FOUR DIAGONALLY STRIPPED SQUARES

1 Sew the two 4" wide lime and white small floral strips to the 1¾" wide pale yellow tonal strips. Press the seam allowance toward the darker fabric.

2 Stitch the two 5¼" wide pink lilac medium floral strips to the other side of the pale yellow tonal strips.

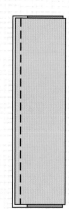

3 Line up the diagonal marking of the 6½" ruler along the seam line to cut two 6½" squares from each stripped unit.

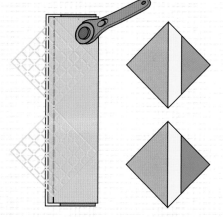

MAKE THE FOUR-PATCH UNITS (CORNERS)

Pair the two 3½" strips of the lime and white small floral with the two 3½" strips of the lilac and rose mini floral/berries, and stitch them together. Press them open, pressing the seam allowance toward the rose/lilac fabric. Subcut eight 3½" wide pieces across the unit. Piece together into four 6½" Four-Patch blocks.

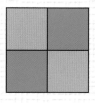

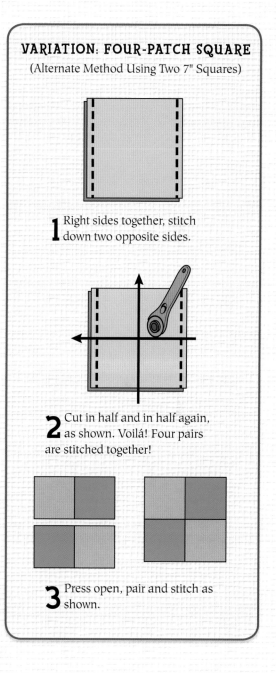

VARIATION: FOUR-PATCH SQUARE
(Alternate Method Using Two 7" Squares)

1 Right sides together, stitch down two opposite sides.

2 Cut in half and in half again, as shown. Voilá! Four pairs are stitched together!

3 Press open, pair and stitch as shown.

Make Half-square Triangle Units

Pair up the following 5½" wide strips:
- Yellow/lime vines with blue/teal medium floral
- Lilac/white small floral with teal/periwinkle mini floral
- Light teal/lilac vine with yellow/white small floral print

Make eight half-square triangle units from each pair of strips according to Method #2 on page 18.

Layout

Position the 6½" squares on a flat design surface, referring to the layout quilt image on page 133 to create the look shown.

Sew

1 Label and sew the squares into columns. This creates seven columns with seven squares in each. Press seam allowances (up for even columns, down for odd columns).

2 Place the flannel backing on a flat surface, right side down, and center the batting on top. Mark the center of this batting/backing unit.

3 Line up the center of Column 4 with the marked center of the batting/backing unit and pin in place.

4 Sew all the columns down (see Sewing the Columns on pages 26–28). Remove postable notes.

Quilt

Quilt your project using contrasting top thread and bobbin thread to match the backing (see Quilting the Project on page 29). Quilt as desired or, starting in one corner, stitch straight across each square, corner to corner, on the diagonal, as shown.

Inner Borders

Add 1⅜" inner pale yellow tonal border strips, courthouse-steps style (see Adding Borders pages 30 and 31), piecing together strips as needed.

Outer Borders

1 Piece one 3½" × 14" strip of the blue/teal medium floral print to each end of two of the 18½" × 3½" lime/blue/yellow floral center border strips. Add to two opposite sides of the quilt, centering the border strip and lining up seams with the seams of the blocks in the central portion of the quilt. Trim.

2 Piece one 3½" × 19" strip of the blue/teal medium floral print to each end of the remaining two 18½" × 3½" lime/blue/yellow floral center border strips. Add these pieced strips to the two remaining sides of the quilt, centering and lining up the seams with the seams of the blocks in the central portion of the quilt. Trim.

3 Add outline quilting to the outer border if desired.

Bind

Trim the backing to 1¼" and the batting to ¼" and complete the self-binding (see Self-Binding on pages 32–35).

ARIADNE'S THREADS

Ariadne was a goddess of Crete as well
as a goddess of the labyrinth, which is
based on the Greek key design shown
here. Her namesake, the human Ariadne,
saved Theseus from certain death at the
hands of the Minotaur by smuggling a
spool of thread to him. As he entered the
Minotaur's lair, Theseus unwound the
thread so he would be able to retrace his
steps out of the maze.

Finished quilt: 31" × 47"
Sample stitched by Sarah Norman of
Sarah's Thimble Quilt Shoppe

FABRIC AND NOTIONS:

- Two fat quarter sets of ten hand-dyed gradations in coordinating light and dark values
- ¼ yd. navy tonal batik (inner border piping)
- ½ yd. coordinating middle-value Bali batik print (border)
- Batting: Crib size (or about 36" × 56")
- 1¾ yds. coordinating flannel (backing/binding)
- Thread for piecing in neutral color
- Thread for bobbin to match backing
- Thread for quilting
- ¼" wide Steam-A-Seam 2 fusible web tape

In This Project:
Starr Design hand-dyed fabric rolls FQ10 Midnight Meadow (lights) and FQ10 Midnight Forest (darks); Sumatra Patina batik by Blank Quilting (borders); navy batik by Island Batik; Tuscany Silk batting by Hobbs; Aurifil thread #3770 for piecing, quilting and topstitching

TOOLS AND SUPPLIES:

- Basic 90-Minute Quilt tools (see pages 8–13)
- 6" × 24" ruler
- 3" square ruler

PREPARE

Prewash the flannel backing and trim to 38" × 58". Prewash other fabrics if desired.

CUT

- Eighty assorted light 3" squares (eight of each; you will use seventy-two)
- Fifty assorted dark 3" squares (five of each; you will use forty-eight)
- Three 2" wide strips of the navy tonal fabric (inner faux piping border)
- Four 4" wide strips of the coordinating middle-value print Bali batik (border)

LAYOUT

Position the squares on a flat design surface, referring to the layout quilt image on page 137 to create the look shown.

SEW

1 Label and sew the squares into columns. This creates fifteen columns with eight squares in each. Press seam allowances (up for even columns, down for odd columns).

2 Place the flannel backing on a flat surface, right side down, and center the batting on top. Mark the center of this batting/backing unit.

3 Line up the center of Column 8 with the marked center of the batting/backing unit, and pin in place.

4 Sew all the columns down (see Sewing the Columns on pages 26–28). Measure frequently to make sure the columns stay centered on the batting/backing unit. Remove postable notes.

QUILT

Any additional quilting is optional.

FLAT-PIPING INNER BORDER

1 Fold and press the three navy tonal strips in half lengthwise, wrong sides together.

2 Trim to ⅞" wide (trim the raw edges, not the folded side).

3 Pin two of the strips along the long unfinished edges of the quilt, lining up the raw edges. Cut the remaining strip in half to create two 21"–22" long strips. Pin them to the short sides. Trim the ends after adding the outer border.

4 Measure the distance between the folded edge of the flat piping and the nearest long seam in several places (as shown) to make sure the two appear parallel.

> Note: Stitching through this border will secure the flat piping. Outline-quilt on the inner edge of the border if desired.

OUTER BORDER

Add the navy tonal batik outer border, courthouse-steps style, adding the sides first, then the top and bottom (see Adding Borders on pages 30 and 31). Trim the flat piping as needed.

BIND

Trim the backing to 3½" and batting to 1¼" and complete the self-binding (see Self-Binding on pages 32–35).

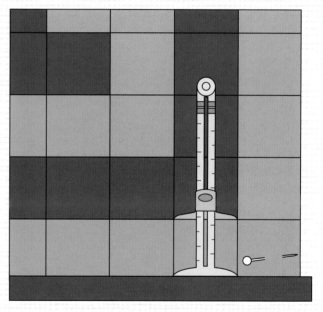

Measure the distance between the folded edges of the flat piping to ensure an even distance all the way around. A locking seam gauge helps achieve quicker and more accurate results.

LAYOUT QUILT

GARDEN TRELLIS

Bring the freshness of the garden inside
with this delightful throw that showcases
those stunning large florals you've been
collecting. Luxurious organic cotton
fleece does dual duty as batting and
backing; it feels divine on cool
evenings when you're dreaming of
warm weather bouquets.

Finished quilt: 58" × 82"
Sample stitched by Gloria Hurban
and Deborah Renfrow

FABRIC AND NOTIONS:

- Twenty-four to forty-eight floral fat quarters in extra-large, large and medium floral prints; Or forty-eight floral fabric pieces at least 6½" × 6½" and four more at least 7½" × 7½"

- Five or more* long quarters or six or more fat quarters of white tonals

- Five or more* long quarters or six or more fat quarters of medium/dark leafy green prints in a range from cool teal to yellow-green

- ⅜ yd. dark green tonal (inner border)

- 1 yd. green/blue watercolor-look fabric (outer border)

- ⅝ yd. blue and green tapestry-look fabric (bias binding)

- 3½ yds. natural color organic cotton fleece (backing/batting) *Note: This will shrink a couple inches. Use natural color because the backing may show through lighter fabrics.*

- Thread for piecing in neutral color

- Thread for bobbin to match backing

- Monofilament thread for quilting**

> * In this sample, I used two extra strips (for a total of seven) in order to create extra half-square triangle units for more options in the design/layout process. **I use MonoPoly monofilament thread because it doesn't tangle.

In This Project:
Flower Mart and Flower Show fabrics, Fossil Fern Sea Crystal (outer border), Damask Blue Green (bias binding), green fabrics for half-square triangles, and Paisley Forest (inner border), all by Benartex; Muslin Mates by Moda; organic cotton fleece by NearSea Naturals; MonoPoly thread by Superior Threads

TOOLS AND SUPPLIES:

- Basic 90-Minute Quilt tools (see pages 8–13)

- 5½" × 24" ruler

- 6½" square ruler with diagonal center markings (for accurate fussy-cutting)

- 7½" square ruler

PREPARE

Prewash and dry the fleece backing. Prewash other fabrics if desired. Piece the backing to 62"/63" × 85"/86". Trim the pieced backing so that the seam is slightly off center (so it won't be overlapped by the pieced seams of the quilt blocks). Press the seam open.

CUT

- Fussy-cut forty-eight 6½" squares from assorted floral fabrics (more may be cut for design flexibility)

- Four 7½" squares from four assorted smaller-scale floral prints (four are required; a fifth square offers more design options)

- Four 7½" squares from a white-on-white/muslin tonal fabrics (four are required; a fifth square offers more design options)

- Eight 5¼" strips from assorted green print fabrics (half-square triangle units)

- Eight 5¼" strips from assorted white tonal print fabrics (half-square triangle units)

- Seven 1½" wide strips from the dark green inner-border fabric (an eighth strip may be needed, depending on the width of your fabric)

- Seven 4" wide strips from the blue/green watercolor outer border fabric

MAKE HALF-SQUARE TRIANGLE UNITS

1 Pair up the 7½" white tonal squares with the 7½" floral squares and make eight half-square triangle units using Method #1 on page 17.

2 Pair up the eight 5¼" wide tonal green strips with the eight 5¼" wide tonal white-on-white strips. Make forty half-square triangle units using Method #2 on page 18. Cut five 6½" squares from each green and white pair.

LAYOUT

Position the squares on a flat design surface, referring to the layout quilt image on page 141 to create the look shown.

SEW

1 Label and sew the squares into columns. This creates eight columns with twelve squares in each. Press seam allowances (up for even columns, down for odd columns).

2 Place the fleece backing on a flat surface, right side down. Mark the center of the backing unit.

3 Position Column 5 on the fleece backing, lining up the left raw edge of Column 5 with the marked center of the fleece backing, and pin in place.

4 Sew all the columns down (see Sewing the Columns on pages 26–28). Remove postable notes.

QUILT

Using monofilament thread in the top thread, stitch in the ditch in horizontal and diagonal seams, backstitching at the beginning and at the end of each. To stitch in the ditch in diagonal seams, follow the long sides of the triangles.

BORDERS

1 Add the inner border, courthouse-steps style, adding sides first, then top and bottom (see Adding Borders on pages 30 and 31). Piece the strips together as needed. The seam allowances on these borders may be pressed open since there is no batting to come through the seam.

2 Add the outer border, courthouse-steps style in the same manner.

3 Quilt the borders if desired (outline-quilt a line around the inner edge of the border).

BIND

Staystitch the perimeter of the quilt within the ¼" seam allowance if desired. Trim and finish the edges with bias binding (see Making/Attaching Bias Binding on pages 36–39).

VARIATION: IN TRAINING

IN TRAINING is made using the same layout as GARDEN TRELLIS and features train motif fabrics.

Train fabrics by Quilting Treasures and Robert Kaufman; Sample stitched by Gloria Hurban

LAYOUT QUILT

AZTEC DREAMS SHAWL

Since ancient times, the Aztec calendar has designated 2012 as the year to herald the beginning of a new era. This elegant shawl features machine-embroidered symbols from the Aztec calendar in jewel-like teal on russet silk, the color of the vibrant earth of pre-Columbian Mexico. Wrap this stunning shawl around a business suit, and these luxurious textures can take any goddess from the office to the opera.

Finished quilt: 29" × 100"
Sample stitched by the author

FABRIC AND NOTIONS:

- about 1¼ yds. 54" wide pumpkin dupioni (embroidered squares; yardage depends on hoop size)
- ⅜ yd. coordinating multicolor cotton/metallic print (squares)
- ¼ yd. 29" wide multicolor silk/rayon brocade (on-point squares)
- ¼ yd. each of seven (or equivalent yardage of four to six colors) tonal teal cotton fabrics (half-square triangle units, on-point squares)
- ¼ yd. each of seven (or equivalent yardage of four to six colors) medium to dark brown batiks and silk dupioni (three brown cottons and four brown dupioni silks were used in this project)
- 3¼ yds. teal silk noil (backing/binding)
- Thread for piecing
- Thread for bobbin to match noil backing
- Teal thread for machine embroidery
- Monofilament thread for quilting*
- ½" wide Steam-A-Seam 2 fusible web tape

*I use MonoPoly monofilament thread because it doesn't tangle.

In This Project:
Silks by Thai Silks; Bali batiks by Robert Kaufman; cottons by Michael Miller, Timeless Treasures and P&B Textiles; Aztec machine embroidery designs from www.trishsthreadsandneedles.com; MonoPoly thread by Superior Threads; clear fabric grabbers from EZ Quilting by Wrights; hot fix crystals and setter by Creative Crystals; Aurifil thread color #5152 (machine embroidery)

TOOLS AND SUPPLIES:

- Basic 90-Minute Quilt tools (see pages 8–13)
- 6" square ruler
- 3½" square ruler
- Fabric grabbers (for ruler)
- Hot fix crystal setter

PREPARE

Wash and dry the teal noil twice to make sure it shrinks and the excess dye is removed. Trim to 36" × 108".

Wash and dry the cottons as desired. Do not wash the silk dupioni or brocade.

CUT

- Ten 6" squares from the multicolor cotton/metallic print
- Seven strips 7" wide from the four to seven teal tonal cotton fabrics (half-square triangle units)
- Seven strips 3½" wide from the four to seven teal tonal cotton fabrics. Subcut twenty-four assorted 3½" squares and twenty-four assorted strips 7" × 3½" (on-point blocks)
- Seven strips 7" wide from the brown silks and cottons
- Twelve 3½" squares from the brocade
- Cut the pumpkin silk dupioni as required to fit your hoop for machine embroidery for twenty-two squares (trim to 6" after embroidering)

Note:
There are four different styles of 6" squares in this shawl:
- Ten squares cut from multicotton/metallic print
- Forty-six brown with teal half-square triangle units made from cottons and silk dupioni
- Twelve squares with silk brocade squares on point, framed in teal cotton
- Twenty-two machine-embroidered silk dupioni squares

MAKE EMBROIDERED SQUARES

1 With teal thread, machine-embroider twenty-two pumpkin silk dupioni squares with Aztec motifs (or other designs of your choice) according to the manufacturer's instructions.

2 Trim the embroidered squares to 6" square.

MAKE HALF-SQUARE TRIANGLE UNITS

1 Pair up the seven teal and seven brown strips, right sides together, as desired. Use at least one cotton strip in each pair.

2 Make forty-six half-square triangle units, using Method #2 on page 18. To inhibit fraying of the silk, zigzag stitch inside each seam allowance before cutting.

> Note: For a similar look without machine embroidering, substitute hand-embroidered dupioni, squares cut from machine-embroidered yardage or fussy-cut motifs from another fancy fabric.

MAKE TEAL SQUARES WITH BROCADE SQUARES ON-POINT

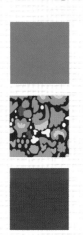 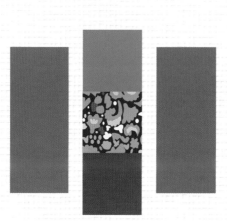 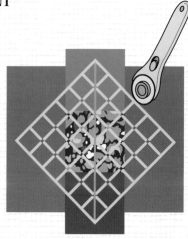

1 Use ¼" seam allowance. Stitch two 3½" teal squares to opposite sides of each brocade square. Chain-sew for speed. Before cutting apart, zigzag stitch within the seam allowance to inhibit fraying. Press the seam allowance so the brocade lies flat.

2 Center two 3½" × 7" teal logs on opposite sides of the three-square unit, and stitch. Zigzag stitch within the seam allowance to inhibit fraying. Press the seam allowance so the brocade lies flat.

3 Use the intersections of ruler markings to center the on-point square inside the 4" square in the ruler. Trim the block to 6" square. Make eleven more blocks like this.

LAYOUT

Lay out the shawl according to the layout image on page 147, placing the half-square triangle units made from all cottons in all four corners.

SEW

1 Label and sew the squares into columns *using ½" seam allowance*. To inhibit the fraying of silk, zigzag stitch inside each seam allowance. This creates eighteen columns with five squares in each. Press seam allowances (up for even columns, down for odd columns).

2 Place the noil backing on a flat surface, right side down. Measuring accurately, mark the center.

3 Position Column 10 onto the backing, lining up the left-hand raw edge of Column 10 with the marked center of the backing, and pin in place.

4 Sew all the columns down (see Sewing the Columns on pages 26–28). Measure frequently to make sure the columns stay centered on the noil backing. Remove postable notes.

QUILT

Stitch in the ditch along the three long seams, using monofilament thread (smoke) on top and thread to match the noil on the bobbin.

BIND

Trim backing to 1¼" and complete the self-binding (see Self-Binding on pages 32–35; omit Steps 3–6).

EMBELLISH

Embellish as desired with hot fix crystals for sparkle and drama!

CONSIDER THIS!

In this project, silks are pieced to cotton, not to other pieces of silk, which alleviates the problem of slippage often associated with stitching silk. In addition, contrasting the luminous sheen of silk with the tonal patterns in the cottons adds textural interest.

Because of the looseness of the weave, silk noil often shrinks noticeably, so always prewash and dry silk noil once or twice before sewing anything that will be laundered later. Some noils will even shrink a bit more on a second laundering. Silk noil can be machine washed on the delicate cycle. For best results, don't overload the washer: this helps keep the fabric from being pulled or stretched. Wash in lukewarm water—never cold or hot. A natural laundry liquid can be better for silk than a soap or detergent. Silk is a protein, so never use bleach, which attacks proteins. Avoid fabric softeners—they clog the silk fibers, reducing breathability. Continued laundering makes noil softer and more supple. Use a medium heat in the dryer so the noil will shrink but not cook, and remove promptly. When pressing, use the silk setting.

CONSIDER THIS!

The Aztec calendar has a twenty-day cycle, and each day is associated with a symbol, called a Day Sign, which gives special significance to the day of one's birth.

For example, the Aztec goddess of love and beauty, and patroness of artisans, Xochiquetzal, is associated with the day sign of the flower, Xochitl.

The face in the center of the Aztec calendar is that of Huitzilopochtli, the hummingbird god. He was immaculately conceived when a bundle of iridescent hummingbird feathers fell from heaven into his mother's heart.

Incorporating personalized elements, such as a symbol associated with the recipient's year of birth, favorite flower or astrological sign, adds a special and appreciated dimension to handmade gifts.

VARIATION: SHAWL MATERIALS

For a different look, this shawl can be made from ninety 6" squares in any combination of cut squares, half-square triangles or Four-Patches, using metallic cottons or other fancy fabrics.

If using thin, polyester brocades, back the fabric with lightweight fusible woven interfacing before cutting squares, and position them next to the cotton squares.

If you don't do machine embroidery, replace the machine-embroidered squares with another fancy fabric that looks like it has or is embroidered or printed with metallic inks, or has fussy-cut motifs from a premium design cotton.

One size fits all! This shawl is great for perking up simple travel outfits and for working gals going out after work. Just throw this elegant accessory over office attire for a glamorous night on the town.

LAYOUT QUILT

TIP TO TRY

If layout space is small, just lay out half of the shawl, using half of the cut squares in equal proportions. Arrange them as desired. Repeat basic positioning for the other side in a mirror image. One way to do this is to place the remaining squares on top of the layout, with right sides together. Pick them up in stacks and label. Alternatively, if you are computer savvy, take a digital photo of the left-hand layout, upload it and flip the image. This gives you a "map" for placement of the remaining squares.

GALLERY

Welcome to a Gallery of Inspiration!
The time-saving methods and clever
designs in these gallery quilts can be
adapted to many other projects, so
have fun inventing new 90-Minute
Quilt variations!

Batikwheel Bounty Lap Quilt
41" × 58"
Stitched by the author

*Six-inch squares make this
attractive quilt quick and easy,
and the simple design allows the
natural beauty of the fabrics to
shine through the design! The
name comes from Island Batik's
Batikwheel Bounty fat quarter set
that was used for the quilt.*

In This Project: Nature-Fil Bamboo
Batting by Fairfield

Grandmother's Heart Quilt
26" × 26"
Stitched by Abby Geddes and Sarah Norman

Nostalgic fabrics remembered from grandmother's quilts add a touch of charm to this heart motif wall hanging. Reproduction fabrics from a variety of bygone eras enhance the "olde tyme" look.

In This Project: Aunt Grace 1930s reproduction fabrics by Marcus Bros, vintage reproduction fabrics by Blue Hill Fabrics; Back to Back's Pacafil alpaca/wool batting; Ro Gregg's Rock 'n Roll flannel by Northcott

Dick and Jane Quilt
31" × 42"
Stitched by the author

Nostalgic fabrics are fun to use, especially when they don't need to be cut up into tiny pieces! More than 85 million Americans learned to read with Dick, Jane and Sally from 1927 through the 1970s in the most popular elementary book series of all time. The Dick and Jane readers were the brainchild of schoolteacher Zerna Sharp (1889–1981). Although she never married, she was affectionately known as the "Mother of Dick and Jane." The fabric collection by Michael Miller even includes Spot the dog, Puff the cat and Sally's teddy bear Tim.

Classic Elegance
24" × 24"

In the collection of Martha Stewart Living Omnimedia

This decorator quilt was made from a Martha Stewart linen collection in order to create a wall hanging to coordinate with the bedroom decor. It hangs by three small plastic drapery rings stitched to the back of the quilt at the corners.

In This Project: Martha Stewart Everyday Linens; Warm Fleece batting by The Warm Company; buttons by www.buttondrawer.com (Photo courtesy of Meryl Ann Butler)

Wedding Keepsake Tablecloth
47" × 47"
Stitched by the author

Forty-nine 6" squares in elegant bridal colors—like tonal cottons, white-on-white muslin, metallics and silks make up this beautiful wedding tablecloth. The thin border adds a touch of color with RJR's Farmer's Market fabrics to symbolize a fruitful life together. Guests signed the borders with their best wishes for the bridal couple, using permanent marking pens.

In This Project: Thermore batting by Hobbs; Sulky Blendables thread #4120 Springtime

Embroidered Victorian Throw

44" × 56"
Stitched and designed by Susan Deal

This opulent throw by author and designer Susan Deal features machine-embroidered dupioni silk squares on a silk noil backing.

In This Project: Silk dupioni from Thai Silks; embroidery designs by OESD; Isacord threads

Sun and Sky Tablecloth

48" × 48"
Stitched by the author

Fussy-cutting, bold fabric designs and clever placement of just sixteen half-square triangle units give this simple quilt an exciting and complex look! An ultrathin batting was used to give the slightest bit of loft.

In This Project: Califon collection by Mark Lipinski's Home for Northcott

The Spectrum of Leadership

33" × 33"
In the collection of Harpo Productions
Stitched by the author

The exciting opening of the Oprah Winfrey Leadership Academy for Girls inspired this quilt. The three squares embroidered with female figures represent the girls in the academy, and the rainbow of color represents the different aspects of leadership these girls will bring to the world stage. The materials used were selected for their appearance as well as for their relationship to the theme of the project. They include:

• Langa Lapu fabrics, hand-dyed with solar-activated dyes made by South African women artisans www.langalapu.co.za

• African Folklore Embroidery squares designed by Ndebele women and stitched with African hand-dyed embroidery floss by Los Angeles–based, South African–native Leora Raikin. The purchase of these embroidery kits supports Ndebele women artists. www.aflembroidery.com

• Beaded motifs made by Capetown mothers with AIDS are used as embellishment. Sales of this beadwork provide the only source of income for these courageous women who do their best to take care of themselves while they tend to their sick children. www.kidzpositive.org

(Photo courtesy of Meryl Ann Butler)

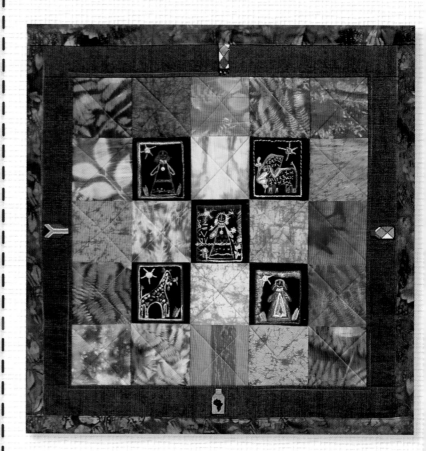

Beatles' Sgt. Pepper Throw

51" × 80"
Stitched by the author

This quilted throw made from an assortment of twelve Beatles motif fabrics and six tonals makes a great gift for those who never left Beatlemania behind. It's perfect for game room, TV room or teen's retro bedroom.

There's a trivia secret in this quilt! There are sixty-four half-square triangle units and sixteen squares in it. Paul McCartney wrote "When I'm 64" when he was 16 years old. The love song is from the Sgt. Pepper album and is the background music for the "Sea of Time" sequence in the movie Yellow Submarine.

In This Project: Beatles (V.I.P Fabrics) and Prism II by Brian Evans for Quilting Treasures; organic cotton fleece from NearSea Naturals (backing)

All-Star Sports

38" × 70"
Stitched by the author

I made a sports-themed lap quilt for each of my three grandsons, Garrett, Trent and Aaron. Both the squares and the backing are cotton flannel, which makes a very cuddly quilt. Many of the same fabrics were used in all three quilts, but each quilt has a unique layout and a different sports-themed flannel backing.

In This Project: Several flannels by Henry Glass; Thermore batting by Hobbs

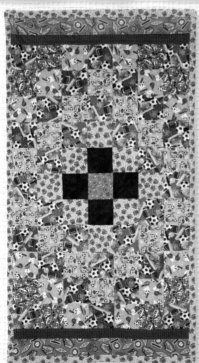

RESOURCES

A.E. Nathan Company
www.aenathan.com
212-686-5194
Fabrics, flannels including extra wide flannels, glow-in-the-dark Halloween print

African Folklore Embroidery
www.aflembroidery.com
818-999-6094
Embroidery kits for quilt squares

Alexander Henry
www.ahfabrics.com
818-562-8200
Fabrics

Aurifil
www.aurifil.com
312-212-3485
Threads

As Cute as a Button
www.ascuteasabutton.com
619-223-2555
Unique buttons

Back to Back Fiber Products
www.backtobackalpaca.com
480-703-2741
Alpaca-cotton and alpaca-wool blend battings

Batik Quilts
www.batikquilts.com
6" kanji squares

Benartex
www.benartex.com
212-840-3250
Fabrics including large scale floral collections, flannels, Minkee microfiber plush

Blank Quilting
www.blankquilting.com
888-442-5265
Fabrics including Yolanda Fundora's Twinkle collection, flannels

Blue Hill Fabrics
877-252-5111
www.bluehillfabrics.com
Fabrics including authentic vintage reproductions

Bonash
www.bonash.com
fiberglass pressing sheet

Brewer Quilting & Sewing Supplies
www.brewersewing.com
800-676-6543
Nifty Notions rulers

The Button Drawer
www.buttondrawer.com
720-434-1090
Unique buttons

Cherrywood Fabrics Inc.
www.cherrywoodfabrics.com
888-298-0967
Hand-dyed suede-look gradation fabrics, Synthrapol

Clover
www.clover-usa.com
800-233-1703
Nancy Zieman 5-in-1 Sliding Gauge (locking), Ultimate Scissors, chalk markers, notions

Creative Crystal
www.creativecrystal.com
800-578-0716
Hot fix crystals and BeJeweler applicator

Creative Grids
www.creativegridsusa.com
419-893-3636
Rulers in a wide range of sizes

Dritz (see Prym)

elinor peace bailey
www.epbdolls.net
360-892-6657
cloth doll patterns, fabric

Fairfield
www.poly-fil.com
Batting, bamboo batting, pillow forms

Fiskars
www.fiskars.com
866-348-5661
Spring-action scissors, rulers

Gingher
www.gingher.com
800-446-4437
Snippers

Henry Glass (see A.E. Nathan)

Hobbs Bonded Fibers
www.hobbsbondedfibers.com
800-433-3357
Battings: Thermore, Tuscany Silk,
Hobbs Heirloom Cotton

Hoffman Fabrics
www.hoffmanfabrics.com
800-547-0100
Fabrics including batiks

Indonesian Batiks
www.indobatiks.com
360-299-3968
6" kanji squares

Island Batik, Inc.
www.islandbatik.com
888-522-2845
Batik fabrics

June Tailor, Inc.
www.junetailor.com
800-844-5400
Notions and rulers

Kona Bay Fabrics
www.konabay.com
800-531-7913
Asian fabrics

LFN Textiles: Artist's Ribbons
www.lfntextiles.com
812-682-373
Jacquard and brocade ribbons

Meryl Ann Butler
www.90minutequilts.com
classes, personal consultations

Michael Miller Fabrics LLC.
www.michaelmillerfabrics.com
212-704-0774
Fabrics, flannels, organic cotton

Moda
www.unitednotions.com
Fabrics, flannels

NearSea Naturals
www.nearseanaturals.com
877-573-2913
Organic threads and fabrics including
cotton and cotton fleece

Northcott
www.northcott.com
201-672-9600
Fabrics, including a wide range of
flannels

P&B Textiles
www.pbtex.com
650-692-0422
Fabric including flannels

Project Linus
www.projectlinus.org
309-454-1764
Charity quilts for kids

Prym Consumer USA Inc.
www.prym-consumer-usa.com
Omnigrid and Omnigrip rulers, Invisi-
Grip, sewing and quilting notions,
Glow-Line tape, Jean-a-Ma-Jig tool

Quilter's Rule
www.quiltersrule.com
800-343-8671
Rulers including nested sets of
graduated sizes

Quilters Dream Batting
www.quiltersdreambatting.com
Battings including recycled and
bamboo/silk/tencel/cotton blend

Quilting Treasures
www.quiltingtreasures.com
800-876-2756
Fabrics, including train fabrics

Quilts for Kids
www.quiltsforkids.org
215-295-5484
Charity quilts for kids

Riley Blake Designs
www.rileyblakedesigns.com
801-816-0540
Fabrics including flannels

RJR Fabrics
www.rjrfabrics.com
800-422-5426
Fabrics, flannels

Robert Kaufman Fabrics
www.robertkaufman.com
800-877-2066
Fabrics including batiks, flannels
and train fabrics

SewBatik
www.sewbatik.com
877-235-5025
Fabrics, flannel batiks (standard and
extra wide widths)

Shaklee Corp.
www.shaklee.com
800-742-5533 (for company
information)
800-530-3305 (for orders)
Shaklee Get Clean Fresh Laundry
Concentrate, Basic H

Simplicity Creative Group
www.simplicity.com
888-588-2700
Rulers, notions, SideWinder, Simpli-EZ
rulers

Starr Design Fabrics, Inc.
www.starrfabrics.com
530-467-5121
Hand-dyed fabric rolls

Sulky
www.sulky.com
800-874-4115
Threads (blendables, Sliver metallics)

Superior Threads
www.superiorthreads.com
800-499-1777
MonoPoly thread, NiteLite ExtraGlow

Sykel (wholesale only)
www.sykelenterprises.com
Licensed collegiate print fabrics

Thai Silks
www.thaisilks.com
800 722-7455
Silks including dupioni, embroidered
dupioni, noil

Timeless Treasures
www.ttfabrics.com
212-226-1400
Fabrics including flannels

Trish Schmiedl's Threads & Needles
www.trishsthreadsandneedles.com
CDs of original embroidery designs
with no jumps, including Aztec Dreams

The Warm Company
www.warmcompany.com
Steam-A-Seam 2, Warm & Natural
batting

Wrights
www.wrights.com
Tassels, rulers, clear fabric grabbers for
rulers by EZ Quilting

Batting Information

for *More 90-Minute Quilts* by Meryl Ann Butler

QUILTING DISTANCE	BATTING	MATERIAL
2"–4" apart	Fusi-Boo Fusible Blended Fiber Batting by Fairfield	Fiber blend including natural cotton and rayon made from bamboo
up to 3" apart	Pacafil Alpaca/Wool	60% Light Alpaca and 40% Wool
up to 3" apart	Pacafil Alpaca/Cotton	Blend of 50% Alpaca and 50% Cotton
up to 4" apart	Tuscany Silk bonded batting by Hobbs	90% silk filaments and 10% polyester
up to 6"–8" apart	Thermore Ultrathin Batting by Hobbs	Polyester
up to 8" apart	Nature-Fil Batting by Fairfield	50% bamboo viscose fiber, 50% organic cotton
	Quilters Dream Cotton by Quilters Dream Batting	100% cotton
	Quilters Dream Orient by Quilters Dream Batting	Blend of bamboo, silk, Tencel, cotton
up to 10" apart	Heirloom Natural with Scrim batting by Hobbs	100% cotton
	Warm & Natural Needled Cotton batting by the Warm Company	100% cotton
up to 12" apart	Dream Green by Quilters Dream Batting	Made from recycled plastic bottles

Ruler Information

for *More 90-Minute Quilts* by Meryl Ann Butler

RULER SIZE	MANUFACTURERS
2.5" × 2.5"	Creative Grid, Fiskars, Olfa, Omnigrid
3" × 3"	Quilter's Rule
3.5" × 3.5"	Creative Grid, Omnigrip
4" × 4"	O'Lipfa, Omnigrid
4.5" × 4.5"	Creative Grid, June Tailor, Olfa, Omnigrid, Quilter's Rule
5" × 5"	Omnigrip, Quilter's Rule
5.5" × 5.5"	Creative Grid, Omnigrip
6" × 6"	Omnigrid, Quilter's Rule
6.5" × 6.5"	Creative Grid, Fiskars, June Tailor, Olfa, Omnigrid, Omnigrip, Quilter's Rule, Simpli-EZ
7" × 7"	Brewer Nifty Notions
7.5" × 7.5"	Creative Grid
8.5" × 8.5"	Omnigrip, Creative Grid
9.5" × 9.5"	Creative Grid, Simpli-EZ
Nested rulers sets (range of sizes)	Quilter's Rule

Note: Always check batting packaging or manufacturers' websites for quilting distance information. These charts are guides only; manufacturers may add or discontinue products.

ABOUT THE AUTHOR

Meryl Ann Butler is an artist, author and educator who has been using the arts as stepping stones toward joyous well-being for the past three decades.

She is the author of the bestseller *90-Minute Quilts: 15+ Projects You Can Quilt in an Afternoon* which she wrote as a "healing-through-creativity" response to the September 11th attacks.

Trained in traditional drawing and painting, Meryl Ann was running her own art school when she took her first quilt class in 1982. Her passion for art and color merged with fiber and texture as she dove headlong into the world of quilting.

Meryl Ann's fiber artwork has been featured in over 100 magazines and periodicals, including *Newsday* and a wide variety of trade publications.

Her quilted art is also in hundreds of collections around the world, including those of His Holiness, the late Swami Satchidananda, the Honorable Nelson Mandela, Cathy and Ed O'Neill, Dr. Caroline Myss, Dr. Barbara King, Dr. Norman Shealy, the Honorable and Mrs. Dennis Kucinich, Harpo Productions, Martha Stewart Living Omnimedia, The Findhorn Community (Scotland), City Hall (Moss, Norway), The St. Petersburg Peace Committee (Russia), School 119 (Odessa, Ukraine) and the University of Peace in Costa Rica.

Visit Meryl Ann at:
www.90minutequilts.com
www.merylannbutler.com

INDEX

MORE GREAT BOOKS FOR FAST AND FUN QUILTS!

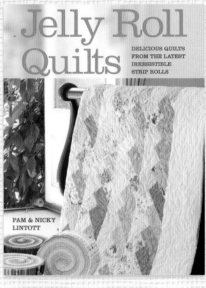

Stash With Splash Quilts

by Cindy Casciato

All quilters have a fabric stash that they don't know how to use. Author Cindy Casciato gives you inspiring quilt patterns to showcase your stash fabrics with a zinger fabric thrown in for splash. Learn time-saving techniques and receive tips from quilting expert Nancy Zieman. An included DVD steps you through a variety of techniques and projects. You'll love combining stash with splash to make these gorgeous quilts!

Paperback, 128 pages + DVD
ISBN10: 0-89689-811-3
ISBN13: 978-0-89689-811-0
Z2918

Sensational Small Quilts

edited by Christine Doyle

With 15 quilt projects plus tips and methods from authors you trust, including Kay Capps Cross and Darlene Zimmerman, you'll learn that small quilts can have big appeal! Break out of the box by tackling modern quilts, attack your stash with beautiful scrap creations, and embrace your heritage with traditional blocks. All quilters will enjoy expanding their technique repertoire with these little quilts.

Paperback, 128 pages
ISBN10: 1-4402-1441-7
ISBN13: 978-1-4402-1441-7
Y0306

Jelly Roll Quilts

by Pam and Nicky Lintott

You'll love making beautiful quilts from those enticing precut strips of fabric known as jelly rolls! One glimpse of a delicious roll of these color-coordinated fabrics and you'll want to make every project inside this book. With names like Pineapple Surprise and Sparkling Gemstones, these 15 delightful quilts are suitable for all skill levels.

Paperback, 128 pages
ISBN10: 0-7153-2863-8
ISBN13: 978-0-7153-2863-7
Z2175

These and other fine Krause Publications titles are available at your local craft retailer, bookstore or online supplier, or visit our website at www.mycraftivitystore.com.